2006 WORLD CUP GUIDE

Editor: Billy Heyman
Sub Editor: Natasha Wladyka
Sales and Marketing: Nick Woodworth (0044 207 287 7053)

Introduction

The Fanfare World Cup guide 2002 has been designed to fit in the pocket of the home based football fan, as well as in the pocket of the lucky few that will be travelling to Japan and Korea. Time zone differences mean that matches will be played at inconvenient times for Europeans and Americans, and we hope that you will be able to use this guide whether you are at home, work or school.

At the time of going to press all information was correct. Please note however that players, managers and websites, have a habit of changing at the last minute and we apologise in advance if you discover any factual errors. Please also note that the capacity listings for the stadiums may vary, as the layout of seating in some of the newer stadiums has still to be exactly confirmed.

We hope you enjoy the World Cup and trust that the Fanfare guide is a useful companion.

Contents

How it all began

It is difficult to believe that the global festival of football that the World Cup is today, began from very humble beginnings and took nearly twenty-six years from idea to fruition. Born from the foundations of a set of rules drawn up by Dutchman Wilhelm Hirschmann, The Federation Internationale Football Association, or FIFA as it is better known, had it's inaugural meeting in 1904. Seven Country members were present: France, Belgium, Spain, Denmark, Holland, Sweden and Switzerland. A basic set of rules were agreed and the members decided that they alone had the rights to organise a World Championship of football.

Plans were put on hold during the decade of the First World War and it was not until 1920 at FIFA's congress meeting in Antwerp that the President and Secretary, Frenchmen Jules Rimet and Henri Delaunay decided that the tournament must go ahead. The 1924 Olympics saw Uruguay win the football gold medal and it was as a result of this that two years later Delaunay again spoke out about the need to start the World Cup. His urgency was borne out of the frustration that professional players were not allowed to compete in the Olympics and teams were suffering as a result.

Uruguay held on to their crown as football Champions in the 1928 Olympics beating Argentina in an all South American final. A month later FIFA met again and the resolution was finally passed for the first World Cup to be played in 1930. The Jules Rimet trophy was sculpted for the winners, 12 inches high, eight pounds of solid gold and finally the stage was set. Now the question on everyone's lips was where would the first World Cup be held?

Uruguay 1930

```
. . Planet Pluto Discovered . . Ethiopian
Haile Selassie Crowned . . Ghandi Indian
Protest . . Great Depression Deepens . .
Nazis Second In Election . . Nylon
Discovered . . Arsenal Win FA Cup . .
Maginot Line finished . .
```

100 year old Uruguay were awarded the title of World Cup hosts as part of their birthday celebrations. But before the party had started, they faced the embarrassing problem of not attracting enough teams. Europe was in recession, Uruguay is a long way away and the centrepiece of the Cup 'The Centenary Stadium' was half finished. Lengthy discussions and negotiation followed but sadly only 13 teams arrived at Montevideo to compete in the first ever World Cup.

The opening game between France and Mexico set the scene for the next fortnight as France ran out 4-1 winners in what was described as a 'lively' game. During the early stages of the competition a league system was used with the group winners qualifying for the semi finals. Hard fought games followed and all the groups were closely contested. But it was Argentina and The US, Uruguay and Yugoslavia who played one another in the semi finals, and by coincidence both games finished 6-1 with Uruguay and Argentina victorious.

The night before the final in Montevideo, thousands of Argentineans poured across the river Plate desperate to get a glimpse of their heroes and see the spectacle that was to be classed as one of the best World Cup finals to date. Home side Uruguay opened their account after 12 minutes with a shot from Dorado that beat keeper Botasso through the legs. Argentina quickly scraped one back and by half time they had doubled their tally with a Stabile goal that the Uruguayans insisted was offside. Revitalised after the break, Uruguay drew level after ten minutes, took the

Official Poster, 1930.

lead after twenty and sealed their World Cup crown with a top corner smash from Castro in the dying seconds. Uruguay were champions and as they paraded the cup around the ground, few would have guessed that they would not be back four years later to defend their title.

Date	Team	HT	FT	Team	HT	FT	Attendance
Final							
30/7/30	**Uruguay**	(1)	4	**Argentina**	(2)	2	93,000
Scorers:	Dorado, Cea Iriarte, Castro			Peucelle, Stabile			

Italy 1934

```
. . Nazi 1000 Year Reich proclaimed . .
USSR Joins League Of Nations . . Mao
Zedong Begins Long March . . Bonnie &
Clyde Killed . . German, Hindenburg Dies
. . Max Baer Heavyweight Boxing Champion
. . Fred Perry wins At Wimbledon . .
Slimming Craze Starts Amongst Women . .
```

The national Italian obsession with Fascism and the spectacular rise to power of leader Benito Mussolini, somewhat overshadowed the second World Cup. The tournament was always intended to be played in a 'non political' arena, but many believed at the time that the Fascists hijacked the tournament and turned it into a media circus. Politics aside, sixteen teams entered: twelve from Europe, one from Africa, one from North America and two from South America. Uruguay decided not to defend their title still reeling after the European lack of support four years earlier.

The competition was initially played out over two rounds. Rounds one and two were a straight knock out followed by semi finals and the final itself.

The layout of the competition meant that after only 90 minutes Brazil, Argentina and the US began their long journey home having been eliminated from the first round. The second round produced semi finalists Italy and Austria along with Czechoslovakia and Germany. Heavily backed Austria, known as the 'Wunderteam' were beaten 1-0 by Italy on a quagmire of a pitch; ironically coach Hugo Meisl was made to eat his words having said only hours earlier that he could win with his reserve team. Much to the annoyance of Mussolini, muscular well-organised Germany were also felled by a skilful, speedy Czechoslovakia 3-1 to set the stage for the first all European final.

The final was played out in Rome in front of a below capacity crowd. Both teams curiously Captained by their goal keepers, endured a turgid first half with alternating possession and few created chances. Puc finally broke the deadlock 20 minutes from time with a Czechoslovakian strike that stunned the crowd to silence. As the minutes crept by, frustration set in with the Italians changing and changing their formation and then by luck rather than judgement eight minutes from time they drew level. A swerving shot from Orsi had ensured extra time. It was to the rapturous delight of the home crowd that in the seventh minute of extra time Schiavia finally sealed it for the Italians. Joyous scenes followed, Mussolini had his win and the sceptics amongst the media questioned whether Italy would have won away from home. Four years later Italy were to be given the chance to finally set the record straight.

Date	Team	HT	FT	Team	HT	FT	Attendance
Final							
10/6/34	Italy	(0)	2	Czechoslovakia	(0)	1	55,000
Scorers:	Orsi, Schiavia			Puc			

France 1938

. . German Anschluss With Austria
Announced . . De Velera Wins Irish
Election . . 'Peace In Our Time'
Declares Chamberlain . . Kuwait
Strikes Oil . . Spanish Civil War . .
Joe Louis Heavyweight Boxing Champion
. . Orsen Welles War Of The World
Book Creates Panic . . Germans March
Into Czechoslovakia . .

War clouds loomed over Europe as France
staged the third World Cup competition of 1938.
Germany had just swallowed Austria in their
Anschluss, absorbing her football team in the
process while civil war continued to rage in
Spain. In all a very dark shadow was cast over
the tournament before a single ball had been
kicked. Nevertheless, sixteen teams entered
the competition but with Austria no longer an
independent state, a spare place was left
unclaimed, giving Sweden a bye into the second
round. Similar to 1934 the tournament took the
unpopular format of a sudden death competition.

Round one produced an amazing game between Brazil and Poland, 4-4 after 90 minutes, Brazil sneaked a 6-5 win after extra time. The tie of round two saw holders Italy take on hosts France in the Colombus stadium in front of 58,000 mostly home fans. Italy won 2-1 in a frantic but well tempered game, which was much in contrast to the butchery that was displayed between Czechoslovakia and Brazil. In a game where Brazil won 2-1, there was a broken leg, broken arm and in total seventeen players were technically injured by the end of the game. Semi finalists Italy, Brazil, Hungary and

Italy's Giuseppe Meazza and Hungary's Gyorgy Sarosi shake hands watched by French referee Georges Capdeville.

Sweden now fought it out for places in the final. Self assured but exhausted Brazil fell to the magnificent technical skill of Italian coach Vittorio Pozzo in a 2-1 win, while Hungary came back to crush the Swedes 5-1 who had surprisingly taken the lead after a mere 35 seconds.

In Paris on the 19th June 1938 the final between Italy and Hungary was played in front of 55,000 spectators. A riveting game followed with Hungary better known for their short passing skilfulness, and Italy for their physical robust

11

approach battling out a six-goal thriller in front of a spellbound crowd. Italy led after six minutes through Colaussi but Hungary were back on level terms only one minute later. Fifteen minutes later Italy led again, but the final nail was firmly hammered into Hungary's coffin as Colaussi smashed home his second 10 minutes before half time to create a 3-1 lead going into the break. Italy were never troubled in the second half and sealed victory with a startling fourth goal ten minutes from the end. Italy had won the World Cup for the second time but with war in Europe, it would be twelve years before they were able to defend their title again.

Date	Team		HT	FT	Team	HT	FT	Attendance
Final								
19/6/38	**Italy**	(3)	4		**Hungary**	(1)	2	55,000
Scorers:	Colaussi (2), Piola (2)				Titkos, Sarosi			

Brazil 1950

. . North Korea March Into South . . Dalai Lama Flees Chinese Invasion . . Russia and China Sign Communist Pact . . USSR Walk Out Of UN . . US & British Troops Fight In Korea . . First Kidney Transplant . . UK Labour Government Win Election . . Petrol Rationing Ends In UK . .

The 1950 World Cup competition in Brazil was beset once again with boycotting countries and with widespread disorganisation. Only thirteen countries entered with notable absences from Argentina, Scotland, France and Czechoslovakia. Germany were still banned after the war and Russia along with Hungary were hiding behind the new Iron curtain. It was against this backdrop of excuses that the gutsy Italians managed to put in a team having lost all of their players one year earlier in the tragic Superga aircrash.

The competition took on a new design with two rounds being played. The first, a basic league system where teams played one another, and the second a final pool of the four group winners with the team with the most points confirmed champions. The first round was deemed absurd by the media. Group four consisted of just two teams: Bolivia and Uruguay, and the remaining groups were furious with the length of travel nations had to endure between matches while Brazil remained static in Rio. The shock of the round saw first time entrants and heavily backed England go down 1-0 to the US, sending them tumbling out of their group and on their way home.

The final pool consisted of Spain, Sweden, Brazil and Uruguay. With 3 games each to play, Brazil convincingly won their first two matches 7-1 and 6-1 against Sweden and Spain, whilst Uruguay managed to beat the Swedes but were forced to a very close draw with the Spanish. Totally unplanned and by coincidence the final game of

13

the tournament was now to decide who were champions. Brazil were heavily tipped to win and amazingly the Governor of the State of Rio announced in front of a 199,854 packed Maracana stadium before kick off that: "..Brazilian players in less than a few hours will be claimed champions.."

The first half of the match was dominated by the majestic Brazilian trio of Zizinho, Ademir and

IV CAMPEONATO
MUNDIAL DE
FUTEBOL
·TAÇA JULES RIMET·

JUNHO DE 1950
BRASIL
Official Poster, 1950.

Jair, who bombarded the goal, forcing spectacular acrobatics from Uruguayan keeper Maspoli. Uruguayan chances were minimal and at half time it would seem that continued pressure would finally break the visitors down. Two minutes after the restart the Brazilians at last breached the Uruguay defences and a huge sense of relief was felt across the stadium. But twenty minutes later the score was level again. After a period of attacking play the equaliser was found by an unmarked Schiaffino and now the game was really on. In the eighty-fourth minute Uruguay put themselves into the history books as Ghiggia settled the match, with a sensational goal. A tense, gripping final five minutes with Brazil camped in the Uruguayan half was not enough though. Uruguay had won the

14

World Cup for the second time and a demoralised Brazil would have four years to lick their wounds before they could try their luck again.

Date	Team	HT	FT	Team	HT	FT	Attendance
Final							
16/7/50	**Uruguay**	(0)	2	**Brazil**	(0)	1	199,854
Scorers:	Schiaffino, Ghiggia			Friaca			

Switzerland 1954

```
. . Dien Bien Phu Falls To Viet Minh . .
Bannister Beats 4 Minute Mile . .
British Troops Pull Out Of Suez . .
Boeing 707 Maiden Flight . . Polio
Vaccine Trials Begin . . Potomac
Agreement Between US and UK . . Bill
Haley Rocks Around The Clock . .
Shocking Lord Of The Flies Published . .
```

The unexpected result of the 1954 World Cup and the drama that preceded it, gives it a place in history as one of the most exciting, exhilarating sporting festivals ever seen. Sixteen teams fought it out in a ludicrously complex new group system, which ensured that the better teams would reach the quarter finals having not been allowed to play one another even if they were in the same group! Germany were back in contention having been banned since the war and the first ever Asian nation Korea, also made their debut appearance.

Round one was not especially closely contested. Hungary scored seventeen goals in their first two games, Uruguay and Austria easily qualified, the former putting seven goals past an absurdly attired Scottish team (they were dressed in full length woollen jumpers in 100 degree heat) while England, Brazil and Yugoslavia qualified as group leaders. The only surprise of the round was to see Italy beaten by Switzerland 4-1 in a playoff game. But the quarter finals were a different story and provided some extraordinary football.

Brazil versus Hungary is still today called 'The battle of the Berne' in recollection of the pitch battle that was fought between the two teams in the dressing room after the match. Eventual winners Hungary (4-2) have English referee Arthur Ellis to

thank for the fact that the game even finished, as player after player were sent off as the cynical tackling went from bad to worse. Other quarter final games of note included a twelve-goal thriller between victorious Austria and Switzerland, a German surprise win against Yugoslavia and a predictable 4-2 win for Uruguay against England. More surprises were evident in the semi final

Brazil's Nilton Santos (L) and Hungary Captain Jozsef Bozsik (R) sent off for fighting.

16

match between favourites Austria and Germany as the Germans romped home 6-1 winners, while in the other semi, Hungary predictably beat Uruguay and the scene was set for a breathtaking final.

The final was played out in front of a packed Wankdorf stadium, which included 20,000 German spectators intent on creating as much noise as possible. Hungary were heavily backed as champions but the question on everyone's lips was whether Puskas would be playing or not. Eight minutes into the game, Hungary were 2-0 up with the partially injured Puskas on the score sheet. But the Germans would not lie down and three minutes later they had pulled one back through a Morlock interception. Minutes before the break the Germans struck again, this time through Rahn, levelling the score and resurrecting their chances. The Hungarians launched attack after attack during the second half, but ten minutes from time they seemed to tire and the Germans upped the pressure. Three minutes later they were in the lead with a low shot from Rahn. The game was now won and as the shockwaves reverberated around the World, the mighty Magyars staggered off the pitch, they had come so close again.

Date	Team	HT	FT	Team	HT	FT	Attendance
Final							
4/7/54	Germany	(2)	3	Hungary	(2)	2	60,000
Scorers:	Rhan (2), Morlock			Puskas, Czibor			

Sweden 1958

```
. . Khrushchev, New Russian Leader . .
Pope John XXII Elected . . European
Economic Community . . US Send First
Satellite to Space . . De Gaulle Elected
French President . . Manchester United
Air Disaster, Stars Dead . . Elvis
Presley Conscripted . .
```

The World Cup is famous for it's ability to produce shock winners, but in 1958 there were no surprises and the best team won. The magnificent Brazil with 17 year old Pele and their new tactical system, injected life into a tournament that was high on formality but often low on excitement. An exhaustive qualification process preceded the start of the World Cup finals and sixteen teams qualified with noticeable absences from Italy, Spain and Uruguay.

The first round consisted of a 4-group league with winners and runners up qualifying for the quarter finals. Defending champions Germany easily qualified in their group and were followed into the next round by runners up Northern Ireland who won a shock playoff game against Czechoslovakia. In the other groups Yugoslavia, Brazil, France and the USSR all qualified at a walk, but Wales had to battle with a weakened Hungary to win their second round place. Hungary had recently emerged from the 1956 anti communist uprising and lost many of their stars; Puskas, Kocsis and Czibor who had all defected. Sadly,

Hungary would never again be the power in football they once were.

The quarter finals were somewhat of an anti climax and the results predictable. Through to the semi finals were Germany with a tough win against the Yugoslavs, France after an easy win against Northern Ireland, Brazil narrowly beating Wales and Sweden with a convincing 2-0 win against the Soviets. Host nation Sweden ensured that they pulled out all the stops for their semi final game against Germany. Cheerleaders whipped up the crowd and initiating a barrage of noise which indisputably assisted Sweden in their 3-1 win having missed many of their earlier chances. Brazil cruised past France with a credible 5-2 win; the astounding Pele scoring a hat trick.

It rained constantly for twenty-four hours before the final and although the Brazilians were heavily backed as winners, the greasy surface was better suited to the Swedes than the skilful Brazilians. Four minutes into the match and without the help of cheerleaders, the Swedes were ahead through Liedholm. Five minutes later the Brazilians were level and by the thirty-second minute they were leading. As the whistle blew for the start of the second half it was obvious that the Brazilians were in their element. Pele flicked the ball into the back of the net in the fifty fourth minute scoring what has been described as the goal of the World Cup. Sweden were not to get back in the game. The final

5-2 score line was a realistic reflection of the match and hailed the beginning of the Brazilian football revolution that would dominate the world for so long.

Date	Team		HT	FT	Team	HT	FT	Attendance
Final								
29/6/58	**Brazil**		(2)	5	**Sweden**	(1)	2	49,733
Scorers:	Vava (2), Pele (2), Zagalo				Leidholm, Simonsson			

Chile 1962

. . Cuban Missile Crisis . . Algerian Independence . . First Orbit Of The World Completed . . Nelson Mandela Jailed . . Polaris Deal Agreed US & UK . . Marilyn Monroe Dies . . Laver Wins Wimbledon . . Sonny Liston Boxing Heavyweight Champion . .

'A country devastated by earthquakes' is how the media of 1961 described Chile. But a year later they had managed to rebuild their country, along with a new stadium in Santiago and put together the framework of organisation that ensured a smooth running tournament. The layout of the competition took on a now familiar structure with sixteen teams in four groups, all playing a league system with the winners and runners up qualifying for the next stage. The only minor change was the introduction of goal difference and the removal of the much aligned playoff game, when points were tied.

The first round and quarter finals will sadly be remembered by the aggressive nature of some of the games and not by the flowing, passing football that was developing within the world game. Dubbed 'The battle of Santiago', Chile beat Italy 2-0 in a first round match but not before two sendings off, a broken nose and much cynical hacking that reduced the game to a pitch battle. An ankle was broken in a Germany/Switzerland encounter and Pele retired injured not to play again in the tournament.

The semi finals saw much-favoured Brazil take on a keen but inferior Chile and the Czechoslovakians take on the Yugoslavians. The European game was hailed: The best defence in Europe against the best attack in Europe, but only 5,890 turned out to watch the Czechs win 3-1 in a scrappy encounter. The largest crowd of the tournament, 76,594, saw Chile fall to the mighty Brazilians in an encounter that ended 4-2 and where the score line was entirely justified.

Brazilian fans carry goal-keeper Gilmar around the national stadium, Santiago.

The tactics of the two finalists were very different and many feared that the Czechs would play a negative game of football and wait for a Brazilian mistake. As it was, Czechoslovakia came straight at Brazil and played some superb football taking the lead in the sixteenth minute with a Masopust strike. Brazil now behind again for a second consecutive final quickly got one back and by half time it remained 1-1. Brazil battled on in the second half and having survived a Czech onslaught in the first fifteen minutes sealed victory with two further goals from Zito and Vava. Brazil had won the World Cup for the second time in succession and the signs were there for a third victory four years later. Few would have believed that in 1966 they would not get through the first round!

Date	Team		HT	FT	Team	HT	FT	Attendance
Final								
17/6/62	**Brazil**		(1)	3	**Czechoslovakia**	(1)	1	68,679
Scorers:	Zito, Vava, Amarildo				Masopust			

England 1966

. . Vietnam War Worsens . . Race Riots In US . . Indian Famine . . Jack Lynch New Irish Leader . . Chinese, Mao Proclaims Cultural Revolution . . Welsh Village, Aberfan 116 Children Dead . . South African Verwoerd Assassinated . . Walt Disney Dies . . Swinging Sixties . .

Seventy countries applied for qualification for the 1966 World Cup finals, and with only fourteen places available as England and Brazil received a bye, they were closely contested. The layout of the tournament remained unchanged with the first match between England and Uruguay kicking off round one. The surprise of the first round had to be the early departure of Champions Brazil. Having beaten the Bulgarians in their opening fixture, they played out one of the games of the finals against Hungary at Goodison Park losing 3-1. North Korea were the other surprise team. Small but very fast and determined, they managed to knock out the Italians at Middlesborough's Ayresome Park much to the delight of their newly adopted English fans.

The quarter final games provided some breathtaking football. England beat Argentina 1-0 in a bad tempered match that saw the South Americans reduced to ten men before half time. Alf Ramsey's players refused to exchange shirts after the match and the media of the day decried the Argentineans as 'Barbaric'. Interestingly, post match analysis showed the English committed thirty three fouls compared to the

Bobby Moore holds up the World Cup.

Argentineans nineteen! An especially physical encounter between the Germans and Uruguayans saw more dismissals with the Uruguayans reduced to just nine men losing 4-0. But the quarter final game of the tournament saw the North Koreans take on the mighty Portuguese and their top scoring sensation Eusebio. 3-0 up after a mere twenty minutes North Korea finally went out 5-3 losers to a Portegese team that would not give up.

The semi final between Russia and Germany has been described as 'best forgotten', while in the other match England beat Portugal in a gripping game that finished 2-1. The final that followed has been portrayed with many adjectives but is best summed up as 'heart stopping'. In front of a packed Wembley stadium, Germany took the lead through Haller after sixteen minutes, but only six minutes later Geoff Hurst equalised for England. The game moved like a pendulum and finally with just minutes remaining Peters broke the deadlock. But the Germans would not lie down and with 15 seconds of normal time on the clock they ensured extra time with a deflected free kick. "..look at them, they're finished.." explained England coach Alf Ramsey as he looked at the exhausted Germans awaiting another thirty minutes of football. Ramsey was right. Geoff Hurst went into the record books as the only hat trick scorer in a World Cup final and England had finally brought the cup home to where the game had been created.

Date	Team	HT	FT	Team	HT	FT	Attendance
Final							
30/7/66	**England**	(1)	4	**Germany**	(1)	2	96,924
Scorers:	Hurst (3) Peters			Haller, Weber			

Mexico 1970

```
. . Peru Earthquake 50,000 dead . .
US Invade Cambodia . . Vietnam War
Stalemate . . Pakistan Typhoon Kills
150,000 . . Northern Ireland Troubles
Escalate . . Heath Wins UK Election .
. Nijinsky Wins Derby. . Monty Python
Flying Circus, Cult Following . .
```

The 1970 World Cup finals had been written off as a disaster before a ball had been kicked. The humidity was too high, the temperature too hot, the facilities inadequate, noon kick off's ridiculous and so the list went on. But above all of this criticism, the tournament proved to be a resounding success. Seventy one countries attempted qualification for the sixteen places. New rules to the competition were two substitutes allowed per game, and also the introduction of the yellow and red card in an attempt to prevent the violence that overshadowed the World Cups of 1962 and 1966. But the most bizarre precursor to the tournament was the war that ensued from a Honduras defeat by El Salvador in the qualification competition. 3,000 people died as a result, all for a game of football!

25

The opening match between Mexico and Russia replicated the curtain riser in 1966 as a sterile goalless draw. But the game of round one is said to have been the meeting of England and Brazil in what has been labelled by some as the 'real final' of the tournament. Brazil were 1-0 winners in a hard fought game that was high on excitement and skill. The quarter finals produced a dour Uruguay/Russia encounter, a rerun of the 1966 final between Germany and England (where this time the Germans won in extra time). Brazil beat Peru 4-2, and an on form Italy beat Mexico 4-1 having fallen one goal behind in front of an especially vocal home crowd.

In an Italy and Germany semi final, a seven-goal thriller was played out. Five goals were scored in extra time and at the final whistle, an exhausted Italy had won by the closest of margins. In the other semi final, Brazil typically came back from 1-0 behind to win 3-1. Unfortunately, the final

is still regarded as a bit of a white wash. Brazil were heavily backed as winners and Italy never really featured in a game that ended 4-1 to

Brazil's Pele celebrates after scoring the opening goal.

Brazil and included goals from the infamous Pele and Jairzinho. Now three times winners of the World Cup, Brazil got to keep it as their own, but interestingly it would be twenty four years before they were entitled to raise it again.

Date	Team	HT	FT	Team	HT	FT	Attendance
Final							
21/6/70	**Brazil**	(1)	4	**Italy**	(1)	1	107,000
Scorers:	Pele, Gerson, Jairzinho, Alberto			Boninsegna			

West Germany 1974

. . India Detonates First Nuclear Bomb . . Turkey Invades Cyprus . . Nixon Resigns As President . . President Ford Sworn In . . Giscard D'Estaing New French President . . Wilson Wins UK Election . . Inflation Hits 20% In UK . . Evert & Connors Win Wimbledon Titles . .

The World Cup continued to grow in popularity with 95 countries entering the qualification process in 1974. England were unsuccessful for the first time, whereas Haiti and Zaire were debutants in a new look competition that hosts West Germany thought would promote attacking football. The new format consisted of 16 teams split into 4 groups with the winners and runners up of a league competition advancing to the next round. Two further groups were formed and the winners then played one another in a final. An additional change to the competition saw a new trophy cast and renamed 'The FIFA World Cup™ trophy', as the original had been awarded to Brazil on a permanent basis in recognition of their three previous wins.

Holland's Johan Cruyff (R) gets ahead of West Germany's Franz Beckenbauer (L).

Holland produced the stylish football of the first round and entertained the world with their 'Total football'. Such was the class of the Dutch team that they employed an interchangeable system where attackers could become defenders and visa versa. Having won two and drawn one game, which included a 4-1 drubbing of Bulgaria, Holland topped their group and advanced to the next stage as favourites. East and West Germany met for the first time, surprisingly the East were the victors, but both managed to qualify for the next stage.

The second round produced some classic games, which included a first time fixture between Brazil and Argentina, Brazil 2-1 victors. Holland totally outplaying a weakened Argentina 4-0, and then beat Brazil 2-0 in a game where Johan Cruyff finally silenced the critics that he was the best player in the world. In the other surviving group, a game between Poland and West Germany was to decide who would appear in the final with both teams having won their earlier matches. Heavy rainfall delayed kick off before a marginally superior West Germany used their home advantage, scraping a 1-0 victory over an unlucky Poland.

Finalists Holland and West Germany battled for the new trophy in front of a capacity crowd at the Munich Olympic stadium and an estimated one billion television viewers. The Dutch were awarded a penalty after a mere sixty seconds and Neeskens ensured their lead. Having settled, the Dutch unwisely began to play complacent, relaxed football and to their dismay, Germany were equal shortly afterwards with a successfully converted penalty. Two minutes from halftime, Muller increased his World Cup goal tally to fourteen and West Germany were now ahead. How Germany survived the ensuing forty-five minutes remains a mystery as Holland launched wave after wave of attack. But it was down to goalkeeper Maier, who played the game of his career and as the final whistle blew Holland knew they had wasted a huge opportunity. Holland are yet to win a World Cup title.

Date	Team	HT	FT	Team	HT	FT	Attendance
Final							
7/7/74	**W. Germany**	(2)	2	**Holland**	(1)	1	77,833
Scorers:	Breitner, Muller			Neeskens			

Argentina 1978

. . Pope John Paul II Appointed . .
Begin Israeli Prime Minister . . First
Test Tube Baby Born . . Iran Under
Martial Law . . Liverpool Win European
Cup For Second Time . . Bjorn Borg
Wins Wimbledon Hat trick . . Lloyd
Webber Musical Evita Smash Hit . .

Argentina had been awarded the position as World Cup hosts of 1978 twelve years earlier at the 1966 finals in London. But in the ensuing years, the country had changed greatly and by the time of the competition, Argentina was a nation ruled by a military Dictatorship, suffering from hyper inflation and an appalling human rights record. It was against this oppressive backdrop that the tournament was governed, which is sadly remembered for the inexcusable standard of refereeing than for the football.

Copying the two-group system of 1974, the first round produced no huge qualification surprises but the second round took on a more coincidental form. Austria, Holland, Italy and West Germany were drawn together in an all European group, while Argentina, Brazil, Peru and Poland formed a predominantly South American group. In a re-run of the 1974 World Cup final, West Germany and Holland competed in an epic match that rightly ended in a 2-2 draw. The winner of the group was decided in the next game though, with Holland and Italy facing one another on the 21st June. With Italy

1-0 ahead at half time thanks to a Brandts own goal, Holland came back to win 2-1 with Brandts redeeming his earlier mistake and securing a place in the final.

In Group B, a turgid 0-0 draw between Argentina and Brazil set the scene for a close and what was to become highly contentious finale. Brazil convincingly beat Poland and Peru and Argentina having also beaten the Poles needed to win by a clear six goal margin to get to the final. What happened next remains one of the talking points of world football. Whether the Peruvians merely surrendered or were bribed remains a mystery. Argentina got their 6-0 win, confirmed their place in the final much to the protests of the Brazilian camp.

The final has been described as 'ill tempered', and the refereeing 'biased and inconsistent'. The game, which ended with an Argentinean victory, should probably have been Holland's for the missed chances and the stroke of luck that is so often needed in such encounters. 1-1 after ninety minutes, extra time produced two Argentinean goals and finally the victory they had prayed for. Joyous scenes followed and for a brief spell Argentina forgot her political and economic troubles. The Dutch licked their wounds; they had come so close again.

Date	Team	HT	FT	Team	HT	FT	Attendance
Final							
25/6/78	**Argentina**	(1)	3	**Holland**	(1)	1	77,260
Scorers:	Kempes (2) Bertoni			Nanninga			

31

Spain 1982

```
. . Israel Invades Lebanon . . Israel
Drive PLO Out Of Beirut . . Gonzalez
Spanish PM . . UK Win Falklands War . .
Polish Solidarity Fight Continues . .
First Artificial Heart Saves Patient .
. Princess Grace Dies In Car Crash . .
ET Film Box Office Sensation . .
```

In a successful bid to encourage third world participation, FIFA decided that for the Spanish 1982 finals there would be 24 places available instead of the usual sixteen. This change meant a new tournament structure had to be designed and the revised layout consisted of six first round groups, with winners and runners up qualifying. The second round was worked on a similar group system with four groups of three teams playing one another with the winners qualifying for the semi finals and then finals.

The opening game of the tournament saw holders Argentina surprisingly beaten by Belgium 1-0, in a dull game where as usual the world media over scrutinised and unsettled the participants. Over the next seven days, new comers El Salvador were thrashed 10-1 by Hungary, Italy narrowly qualified for the next round having been held to 1-1 draw by Cameroon, while England and Brazil easily qualified from their groups with maximum points.

The highlights of the second round were numerous. Brazil were brilliant against Argentina, beating them 3-1 after Maradona had been sent off.

They then played Italy but fell to a majestic Paolo Rossi hat trick. France won both of their games and West Germany ensured England's departure with a goalless draw. The semi final game between France and Germany is best described as thrilling. The game see-sawed to extra time and survived the further thirty minutes both teams with three goals. Germany held their nerve to win the penalty shoot out 5-4 and a place in the final. In the other semi final Poland missed their suspended striker Boniek and lost 2-0 to Italy.

Lacking any form of shape and cohesion, the opening half of the final was punctuated with fouls and hard tackling. But it was in the second half that the game that had promised so much began to come to life. Italy took the lead with a Rossi strike eleven minutes into the half, and then doubled their advantage twelve minutes later. The game was now theirs but Germany ran forward desperate to score, and in the process exposed a gap that was exploited by the Italians who were finally victorious. Veteran, legend and goalkeeper Dino Zoff collected the World Cup trophy and Italy joined Brazil as the only team with three World Cup titles to their name.

Date	Team	HT	FT	Team	HT	FT	Attendance
Final							
11/7/82	Italy	(0)	3	Germany	(0)	1	90,000
Scorers:	Rossi, Tardelli, Altobelli			Breitner			

Mexico 1986

. . Challenger Space Shuttle Disaster . .
Olof Palme Swedish PM Shot Dead . . Marcos
Flees, Aquino In Power . . Chernobyl
Disaster . . South Africa Declare State Of
Emergency . . Tyson 20 Year Old Heavyweight
Champion . . Aids Health Shock . .

Second time hosts Mexico endured the
numerous complaints about the tournament which
included heat, humidity, altitude and the lack of
oxygen, to produce one of the best World Cup finals
for decades. It was to be the competition where one
player was so influential in the outcome of the
games that some even say 'single handedly' won
the cup for Argentina. Mexico 1986 will always be
remembered as Maradona's World Cup. As in 1982,
twenty four teams competed in a slightly revised
tournament where the second round of groups were
replaced by a straight knock out. With the first round
producing some surprises, Brazil and Denmark were
the only two teams to qualify for the second round
with maximum points.

The second round knock out phase was
packed with drama and excitement. Argentina V
Uruguay is always viewed as a derby game when
the potentially explosive ingredients are mixed.
But with some excellent refereeing, tempers were
controlled and Argentina went on to win 1-0. France
knocked out Italy 2-0, England cruised past
Paraguay 3-0 but the clash of the round saw an

extra time seven-goal thriller between Belgium and Russia, with Russia on the losing end. The quarter finals now produced two intriguing ties. England, Argentina and Brazil versus France.

The fallout of the Falklands conflict did not help the build up to the Argentina quarter final, but it was a reversal in fortunes that saw Argentina take the semi final place with a 2-1 win in the now infamous game. Maradona scored once with his hand and once with his feet, beating three defenders before rounding keeper Peter Shilton in what has often been referred to as the best ever World Cup goal. France and Brazil were unable to break their 1-1 deadlock and were forced to a penalty shoot out, France winning 4-3.

Both semi final games curiously ended 2-0, Maradona again scoring twice to brush aside Belgium, while Germany made light work of an exhausted French team. The final was to be a breathtaking spectacle, Argentina taking the lead and then doubling their advantage in the fiftieth minute. But the Germans would not lie down and they soon found themselves level thanks to goals from Voller and Rummenigge. But it was to be Argentina's

Argentina's Maradona with the cup after their victory over West Germany in the 1986 final.

35

day. Six minutes from time, Burruchaga sealed victory and the jubilant Argentineans carried the World Cup home for the second time.

Date	Team	HT	FT	Team	HT	FT	Attendance
Final							
29/6/86	**Argentina**	(1)	3	**Germany**	(0)	2	114,590
Scorers:	Brown, Valdano, Burruchaga			Rummenigge, Voller			

Italy 1990

. . Nelson Mandela Free . . 40,000 Die In Iran Earthquake . . Poll Tax Riots Shake London . . Iraq Invades Kuwait . . Force Build Up In Saudi Arabian Desert . . Thatcher Resigns . . Major New UK PM . . USSR Dissolves . . Hubble Telescope Launched . . Manchester United Win FA Cup . .

Italy 1990 is often remembered as an over defensive tournament that was marred by a loathsome bad tempered final. Second time hosts Italy decided to stick with the 1986 tournament format, which included the successful introduction of second round knock out rather than a more laborious league system. Newcomers included Ireland managed by World Cup winner Jackie Charlton and Costa Rica, a team that would shake Scotland to its core with a 1-0 win in the opening game.

The first round saw a surprise win for Cameroon against Argentina. Thirty eight year old Roger Milla was still playing for Cameroon and it was his style and the team's outlandish often unpredictable nature that gained them so many neutral supporters. But it was the second round that produced some of the most spectacular football. Cameroon squeezed past Colombia while Brazil amazingly lost 1-0 to Argentina having hit the woodwork three times and claiming 80 % of the posession. In a fearsome encounter Germany won against Holland but not before both teams had a man sent off; Voeller and Rijkaard for spitting! Both England and Ireland qualified. England thanks to a spectacular David Platt volley in the dying seconds against Belgium, and David O'Leary for Ireland with the final penalty in a forced shootout.

In the final eight, a depleted Cameroon with four suspensions entertained the world losing a 3-2 thriller against a slightly superior England. Ireland who had been adopted by the American home crowd finally succumbing to an Italian team that would not give up. The semi finals produced an interesting but cruel conundrum as both games ended in 1-1 draws after one hundred and twenty minutes. Penalty shootouts followed with Argentina and Germany victors in a sad decider to the greatest football tournament in the world.

Argentina with four players suspended were intent on playing a defensive game for the first half of the final. The German midfield pushed the game forward desperate to find their strikers but to little avail. In the sixty fifth minute Argentinean Monzon was sent off and the inevitable now seemed set to happen.

Continued German pressure forced a dubious penalty five minutes from time and Brehme made no mistake. The game was won. Maradona's refusal to shake the hand of the FIFA president while collecting his runners up medal was the icing on the cake of a final that is probably best forgotten.

Date	Team	HT	FT	Team	HT	FT	Attendance
Final							
8/7/90	**Germany**	(0)	1	**Argentina**	(0)	(0)	73,603
Scorers:	Brehme						

USA 1994

. . Bosnia War Thousands Dead . .
Thousands Die In Rwanda Massacre . .
Mandela Elected In First Elections .
. Russians Attack Chechnya . .
Ceasefire In Northern Ireland . .
Major League Baseball Players Strike
. . Sampras Wimbledon Glory . . OJ
Simpson Arrested . .

Association football has never been the American's favourite sport; in fact it sits a poor fourth place behind American football, baseball and basketball. It was thus quite a surprise to the world that the USA were awarded the finals especially when you include the huge distances between venues along with the searing heat. The tournament however was well natured and regarded by many as a huge success. After an appalling opening ceremony the crowds turned up, the refereeing was much improved by FIFA, and the first round was in some cases very very close.

A record 141 nations entered the qualification race for 24 places, Maradona made a comeback from retirement before being forced back home for banned substance abuse, and during the first round, all of group E finished level on points. The second round shock saw a Hagi led Romania knock out Argentina 3-2, a score line that flatters Argentina such was the scope of the victory. Ireland made two poor defensive errors and paid the price to the Dutch. Italy narrowly beat Nigeria and the US were unable to use the fourth of July to their advantage, knocked out 1-0 by a sluggish Brazil.

Holland versus Brazil was by far the most entertaining of the last eight games. After a dull goalless draw in the first half a five-goal thriller followed with a

Italy's Roberto Baggio disappointed after missing his penalty but Brazil celebrate.

Brazilian free kick sealing victory, minutes from time. The semi finals were turgid, Bulgaria seemed happy to have reached the last four as they were brushed aside 2-1 by Italy. In the second semi final an over defensive Sweden were reduced to ten men before Romario sealed a Brazilian win.

The Final was dull beyond belief. The only interesting statistic was that one of the teams were destined to a fourth World Cup victory, but sadly the way in which it was done was via a penalty shoot out. One hundred and twenty minutes of football could not decide a winner. Both teams were absolutely exhausted, Italy having crossed four time zones to reach the final and Brazil also had endured a similar amount of travel over the previous month. Roberto Baggio has the unfortunate stigma of missing the penalty that sealed victory for Brazil. It was a sad end to a well-organised tournament.

Date	Team	HT	FT	Team	HT	FT	Attendance
Final							
17/7/94	Brazil +	(0)	0	Italy	(0)	0	94,194

+ After extra time Brazil win on penalties

France 1998

. . Fighting In Kosovo . . Pinochet
Arrested In London . . White House
Sex Scandal, Clinton Shame . . Good
Friday Agreement Reached In Northern
Ireland . . Euro Currency Agreed . .
Denver Beat Green Bay at Superbowl . .
Titanic Movie Breaks All Records . .

Twelve additional teams were given places in the World Cup finals of 1998, in a bid to make the World Cup a truly global contest that until now had been dominated by Europe and South America. In an attempt to reduce the number of penalty shootouts during the later stages of the competition, a new rule called 'the golden goal' was introduced. Often controversial, the rule stated that the first goal scored during extra time would win the game. Travel between games was evenly spread, and it was felt for the first time that teams would suffer the fatigue from air travel equally.

Round one saw Spain and Italy exit early, but again it was the second round where some of the very best football was contested. Lauren Blanc made World Cup history scoring the first ever 'golden goal' against a credible Paraguay who had held the match to a goalless draw, before extra time. Holland narrowly beat Yugoslavia with a late free kick while Brazil brushed aside Chile 4-1. But the game of the round was between Argentina and England. With the score 2-2 at half time, England were reduced to ten men minutes later, but they somehow managed to hang on with the game now forced to a penalty shoot out. Argentina shot straighter and confirmed their place against Holland in the next round.

Croatia were now quarter finalists in their first ever World Cup appearance and further showed their pedigree by beating a ten man Germany 3-0. Croatian striker Suker scored in the victory and was later to be awarded the 'Golden Boot' trophy as the tournaments top scorer. In another nail biting game, Holland knocked out Argentina 2-1 while Italy lost on penalties to a lucky France. A penalty shootout was used again, this time to decide the semi final game between Brazil and Holland. Brazil were winners and it was not long before France joined them as finalists

The France team celebrate after beating Brazil 3-0 in the final at the Stade de France in Paris.

having beaten Croatia 2-1 with only ten men.

In the hours before the final, Brazilian phenomenon Ronaldo was struck down and briefly hospitalised with a seizure. What happened next has never become clear. Statements were made to suggest he was playing and then were denied, but all was confirmed as a haggard looking Ronaldo took to the pitch to face the French, a mistake that would cost the Brazilians the game. France were the superior team from the kick off. They hounded the Brazilians with a quick passing, brisk game and by the twenty seventh minute they were ahead. Three minutes later Zidane made it two for France and two for himself. The Brazilians laboured through the second half never looking likely to score, but it was in extra time that Petit put the final nail in the coffin making it 3-0. France, the architects of the World Cup competition had won the tournament for the first time.

Date	Team	HT	FT	Team	HT	FT	Attendance
Final							
12/7/98	France	(2)	3	Brazil	(0)	0	75,000
Scorers:	Zidane (2), Petit						

42

Argentina

Capital City:
Buenos Aires

Location: Located on the Southern tip of South America, Argentina borders Chile to the West and Uruguay, Paraguay, Brazil and Bolivia to the North and East

Land Mass: 2,780,000 Km Sq

Average monthly income US Dollars: $630 Per Month

Currency: 1 Peso = 100 Centavos

Population: 36 Million

Football in Argentina:

Year Football Federation was founded: 1893

Number of registered football clubs: 3,035

Number of registered players: 306,365

Official website address: www.afa.org.ar

National colours: Light blue and white striped shirts, black shorts and white socks

43

Previous World Cup Finals Experience:

Previous World Cup finals appearances: 1930, 1934, 1958, 1962, 1966, 1974, 1978 (Hosts), 1982, 1986, 1990, 1994, 1998

Best position in the finals: Winners 1978, 1986

Largest victory in the finals: 6-0 V Peru, 1978

Heaviest defeat in the finals: 1-6 V Czechoslovakia, 1958

Highest attendance in the finals: 114,590 V West Germany, 1986

Lowest attendance in the finals: 1,000 V Chile, 1930

How Argentina qualified for the World Cup Finals:

How did the qualification process work in Argentina's continent?

10 South American countries applied for qualification and played each other at Home and Away on a league basis. The first 4 countries gained automatic qualification with the fifth placed team playing the winner of the Oceania group at Home and Away (Uruguay V Australia).

Final Position in their group table:

Country	Pl	W	D	L	F	A	GD	Pts
Argentina	18	13	4	1	42	15	27	43
Ecuador	18	9	4	5	23	20	3	31
Brazil	18	9	3	6	31	17	14	30
Paraguay	18	9	3	6	29	23	6	30
Uruguay	18	7	6	5	19	13	6	27
Colombia	18	7	6	5	20	15	5	27
Bolivia	18	4	6	8	21	33	-12	18
Peru	18	4	4	10	14	25	-11	16
Venezuela	18	5	1	12	18	44	-26	16
Chile	18	3	3	12	15	27	-12	12

The 2002 Argentina World Cup Team:

Name of the Coach: Marcela Biesla

World ranking (January 2002): 2

Approximate betting odds: 4/1

Drawn in Group: F

Country where they will play the group matches: Japan

Players to watch: Gabriel Batistuta, Hernan Crespo, Juan Sebastian Veron

Overview of Argentina:

It is very difficult to say who the favourite is between France and Argentina for the World Cup 2002 trophy, but one thing is for sure. The draw has ensured that they are not able to meet in the final at Yokohoma, and they may even meet as early as the second round, if at all. Twice World Cup winners and twice runners up, Argentina showed their pedigree and supreme consistency in the qualification rounds. Over 18 games they lost only once (to old rivals Brazil), drew 4 and won the remaining 13 games amassing a 12 point gap to the second team in their group, Ecuador. Players to watch out for are numerous: Batitstuta, Veron, Crespo, Sorin, Ortega, Gonzalez, Zanetti, all players that would grace just about any international team even on an off day. Coach Biesla will predictably be playing his 3-3-2-2 system. He will be hoping that in the second game against England they will win outright, this time avoiding the penalty shootout.

Belgium

Capital City: Brussels

Location: West European Nation located between the Netherlands, Germany, Luxembourg and France

Land Mass: 30,540 Km Sq

Average monthly income US Dollars: $2,054 Per Month

Currency: 1 Euro = 100 Cents

Population: 10 Million

Football in Belgium:

Year Football Federation was founded: 1895

Number of registered football clubs: 2,120

Number of registered players: 390,468

Official website address: www.footbel.com

National colours: All red, with yellow and black trim on collar

Previous World Cup Finals Experience:

Previous World Cup finals appearances: 1930, 1934, 1938, 1954, 1970, 1982, 1986, 1990, 1994, 1998

Best position in the finals: Fourth 1986

Largest victory in the finals: 3-1 V Uruguay, 1990

Heaviest defeat in the finals: 2-5 V Germany, 1934

Highest attendance in the finals: 114,000 V Argentina, 1986

Lowest attendance in the finals: 900 V Paraguay, 1930

How Belgium qualified for the World Cup Finals:

How did the qualification process work in Belgium's continent?

51 European Countries entered the qualifications; France were given an automatic qualification place for winning the 1998 World Cup and the remaining 50 teams were split into 4 groups of 5 teams and 5 groups of 6 teams. The group winners were all awarded automatic qualification with the 9 Runners up playing one another with the exception of 1 team (Ireland) who played the winning Runner up of the Asian qualification group (Iran).

Final Position in their group table:

Country	Pl	W	D	L	F	A	GD	Pts
Croatia	8	5	3	0	15	2	13	18
Belgium	8	5	2	1	25	6	19	17
Scotland	8	4	3	1	12	6	6	15
Latvia	8	1	1	6	5	16	-11	4
San Marino	8	0	1	7	3	30	-27	1

The 2002 Belgium World Cup Team:

Name of the Coach: Robert Waseige

World ranking (January 2002): 20

Approximate betting odds: 50/1

Drawn in Group: H

Country where they will play the group matches: Japan

Players to watch: Walter Baseggio, Emile Mpenza, Marc Wilmots

Overview of Belgium:

Belgium qualify for their sixth successive finals after meeting the Czech Republic in the European playoffs and winning 2-0 on aggregate. The first round draw in December was favourable to the Flemish but they are holding back any immediate celebrations as they are only too aware how the expected can so easily become the unexpected.

49

The European Championships of 2000 and France 1998 saw Belgium exit in the first round and both times by a small margin. They will be hoping that Striker Emile Mpenza who plies his trade at Schalke 04 (German Bundesliga) and veteran Marc Wilmots will be able to set the record straight taking them directly to the second round. An opening match against the Japanese in front of 64,000 home fans will be a stern first test, but the 'Diables Rouges' seem quietly confident that they can spoil the party.

Brazil

Capital City: Brasilia

Location: Consisting of a third of the South American continent, Brazil is located in the East and centre of the continent

Land Mass: 8,511,965 Km Sq

Average monthly income US Dollars: $362 Per Month

Currency: 1 Real = 100 Centavos

Population: 170 Million

Football in Brazil:

Year Football Federation was founded: 1914

Number of registered football clubs: 12,987

Number of registered players: 551,358

Official website address: www.brasilfutebol.com

National colours: Yellow shirts with green collars and cuffs. Blue shorts and white socks with green-yellow border

51

Previous World Cup Finals Experience:

Previous World Cup finals appearances: 1930, 1934, 1938, 1950 (Hosts), 1954, 1958, 1962, 1966, 1970, 1974, 1978, 1982, 1986, 1990, 1994, 1998

Best position in the finals: Winners 1958, 1962, 1970, 1994

Largest victory in the finals: 7-1 V Sweden, 1950

Heaviest defeat in the finals: 1-4 V Hungary, 1954

Highest attendance in the finals: 199,854 V Uruguay, 1950

Lowest attendance in the finals: 1,200 V Bolivia, 1930

How Brazil qualified for the World Cup Finals:

How did the qualification process work in Brazil's continent?

10 South American countries applied for qualification and played each other at Home and Away on a league basis. The first 4 countries gained automatic qualification with the fifth placed team playing the winner of the Oceania group at Home and Away (Uruguay V Australia).

Final Position in their group table:

Country	Pl	W	D	L	F	A	GD	Pts
Argentina	18	13	4	1	42	15	27	43
Ecuador	18	9	4	5	23	20	3	31
Brazil	18	9	3	6	31	17	14	30
Paraguay	18	9	3	6	29	23	6	30
Uruguay	18	7	6	5	19	13	6	27
Colombia	18	7	6	5	20	15	5	27
Bolivia	18	4	6	8	21	33	-12	18
Peru	18	4	4	10	14	25	-11	16
Venezuela	18	5	1	12	18	44	-26	16
Chile	18	3	3	12	15	27	-12	12

The 2002 Brazil World Cup Team:

Name of the Coach: Luiz Felipe Scolari

World ranking (January 2002): 3

Approximate betting odds: 8/1

Drawn in Group: C

Country where they will play the group matches: South Korea

Players to watch: Rivaldo, Roberto Carlos, Denilson, Ronaldo

Overview of Brazil:

4 times World Champions and finalists in France
98, Brazil have not been at their best of late.
Losing 6 of their 18 qualification matches, using 59
players and three managers, the Brazilians finally
qualified third in their group. Their first round draw
has been described as a dream, as even an off
form Brazil should fare well against Costa Rica
and China. With a team packed full of talent,
Scolari's recent problems may have been caused
by too much choice; Rivaldo (footballer of the year
1999), Roberto Carlos, Denilson, Ronaldo,
Romario and many others prove Brazil's pedigree.
As an 8/1 shot, the momentum gained in the first
round could be the start Brazil need to propel them
into the final stages.

Cameroon

Capital City: Yaounde

Location: Located in Western Africa, Cameroon is bordered by Nigeria to the North and West, Chad and the Central African Republic to the East, Congo, Gabon and Equatorial Guinea to the South and the Atlantic Ocean to the West

Land Mass: 475,442 Km Sq

Average monthly income US Dollars: $50 Per Month

Currency: 1 CFA Franc = 100 Centimes

Population: 16 Million

Football in Cameroon:

Year Football Federation was founded: 1959

Number of registered football clubs: 200

Number of registered players: 9,328

Official website address: None Known

National colours: Green shirts, red shorts and yellow socks

Previous World Cup Finals Experience:

Previous World Cup finals appearances: 1982, 1990, 1994, 1998

Best position in the finals: Quarter Finals 1990

Largest victory in the finals: 2-1 V Romania, 1990, V Colombia, 1990

Heaviest defeat in the finals: 1-6 V Russia, 1994

Highest attendance in the finals: 83,959 V Sweden, 1994

Lowest attendance in the finals: 11,000 V Peru, 1982

How Cameroon qualified for the World Cup Finals:

How did the qualification process work in Cameroon's continent?

50 African teams signed up for the World Cup qualification and 5 places were allocated. 2 Rounds of games were played with Round 1 being a two leg competition (Home and Away) between two countries. The Aggregate winners of Round 1 were then entered into the second Round. The second Round was a simple 5 group league system with the group leaders after eight games qualifying.

Final Position in their group table:

Country	Pl	W	D	L	F	A	GD	Pts
Cameroon	8	6	1	1	14	4	10	19
Angola	8	3	4	1	11	9	2	13
Zambia	8	3	2	3	14	11	3	11
Togo	8	2	3	3	11	13	-2	9
Libya	8	0	2	6	7	20	-13	2

The 2002 Cameroon World Cup Team:

Name of the Coach: Winfried Schafer

World ranking (January 2002): 38

Approximate betting odds: 33/1

Drawn in Group: E

Country where they will play the group matches: Japan

Players to watch: Patrick Mbomba, Lauren, Samuel Eto'o

Overview of Cameroon:

The Indomitable Lions - Cameroon. World Cup quarter finalists in 1990, holders of the African Nations Cup and Sydney 2000 Olympic gold medallists. Cameroon qualify for the fifth time (a record for an African Nation) as group winners having only lost one match. The team boasts a number of quality players, the modest Patrick Mbomba (currently African footballer of the year), Lauren (African Nations player of the tournament 2000), Rigobert Song of West Ham (English Premiership), Real Madrid's Njitap and Samuel Eto'o. Winfried Schafer the coach will face his home country Germany on the 11th June, and with Ireland and Saudi Arabia in the same group he claims they are the best placed African Nation to reach the second stage. Sadly, Roger Milla will not be with the team. He made his final appearance at the age of 42 (1994) and having recently been voted the African player of the century, many claim it is he who put Cameroon on the map as a footballing nation.

China

Capital City: Beijing

Location: The third largest country in the world, China is bounded to the North by the deserts of Mongolia, to the West by the Tibetan plateau and the Himalayas, and to the East by the East and South China seas

Land Mass: 9,597,000 Km Sq

Average monthly income US Dollars: $65 Per Month

Currency: 1 Yuan = 10 Jia = 100 Fen

Population: 1.3 Billion

Football in China:

Year Football Federation was founded: 1924

Number of registered football clubs: 1,045

Number of registered players: 2.25 Million

Official website address: www.fa.org.cn

National colours: White shirt with red stripes on shoulder, white shorts and socks

Previous World Cup Finals Experience:

Previous World Cup finals appearances: China appear in the World Cup finals for the first time

How China qualified for the World Cup Finals:

How did the qualification process work in China's continent?

39 Countries entered the qualifications (Japan and South Korea were given a bye as host nations) and played Round 1 in a ten league competition with the winners of each league going forward into the second round. The second round consisted of two Leagues of 5 teams with the winners automatically qualifying and the Runners up playing each other (Iran V UAE). The winning Runner up (Iran) then played the European Runner up of Group 2 (Ireland) for the final position.

Final Position in their group table:

Country	Pl	W	D	L	F	A	GD	Pts
China	8	6	1	1	13	2	11	19
UAE	8	3	2	3	10	11	-1	11
Uzbekistan	8	3	1	4	13	14	-1	10
Qatar	8	2	3	3	10	10	0	9
Oman	8	1	3	4	7	16	-9	6

The 2002 China World Cup Team:

Name of the Coach: Bora Milutinovic

World ranking (January 2002): 55

Approximate betting odds: 250/1

Drawn in Group: C

Country where they will play the group matches: South Korea

Players to watch: Ma Mingyu, Fan Zhiyi, Li Tie

Overview of China:

The road to qualification has been a long one for China, almost 45 years have passed since they first entered the qualifying stages in 1957. An estimated influx of 500,000 visiting fans have delighted the South Koreans and the 500 Million extra television viewers will bump up advertising revenues. It would seem that China's win against Oman in September was more significant than first thought. The introduction of coach Milutinovic ('Bora' to his many fans), was a considerable factor in qualification. He has a wealth of experience having coached and qualified with Mexico (1986), Costa Rica (1990), United States (1994) and Nigeria (1998). The current ban on the export of Chinese players under 28 has not helped them gain worldwide experience, but Dundee's Fan Zhiyi and veteran Ma Mingyu will no doubt be leading from the front. Youngsters to look out for include Li Wei Fe, Jiang Jin and Li Tie. With odds of 250/1 and the prospect of facing Brazil on the 8th June, China must simply be pleased to have arrived.

Costa Rica

Capital City: San Lose

Location: A Central American Country that lies between Nicaragua to the North and Panama to the South

Land Mass: 51,100 Km Sq

Average monthly income US Dollars: $298 Per Month

Currency: 1 Costa Rican Colon = 100 Centimos

Population: 3.7 Million

Football in Costa Rica:

Year Football Federation was founded: 1921

Number of registered football clubs: 431

Number of registered players: 12,429

Official website address: www.intnet.co.cr/sports/fedefutbol/fede.htm

National colours: Red and white shirts, blue shorts and white socks

Previous World Cup Finals Experience:

Previous World Cup finals appearances: 1990

Best position in the finals: Second Round, 1990

Largest victory in the finals: 2-1 V Sweden, 1990

Heaviest defeat in the finals: 1-4 V Czechosolvakia, 1990

Highest attendance in the finals: 47,673 V Czechoslovakia, 1990

Lowest attendance in the finals: 30,223 V Sweden, 1990

How Costa Rica qualified for the World Cup Finals:

How did the qualification process work in Costa Rica's continent?

The CONCACAF (Confederation of North Central American and Caribbean Association Football) was probably the most complicated and extensive qualification process. There were three qualification stages - the preliminary phase, the semi finals and the final qualification stage. The phases were run on a league basis with Costa Rica, Jamaica, Mexico and USA all getting byes from the first stage having qualified for the World Cup finals before. The final group of six played home and away with the top three in the group qualifying.

Final Position in their group table:

Country	Pl	W	D	L	F	A	GD	Pts
Costa Rica	10	7	2	1	17	7	10	23
Mexico	10	5	2	3	16	9	7	17
USA	10	5	2	3	11	8	3	17
Honduras	10	4	2	4	17	17	0	14
Jamaica	10	1	2	7	5	18	-13	5
Trinidad	10	1	2	7	5	18	-13	5

The 2002 Costa Rica World Cup Team:

Name of the Coach: Alex Guimares

World ranking (January 2002): 31

Approximate betting odds: 200/1

Drawn in Group: C

Country where they will play the group matches: South Korea

Players to watch: Hernan Medford, Paulo Wanchope, Rolando Fonseca

Overview of Costa Rica:

Costa Rica qualify for the World Cup for the second time. The Ticos as they are universally known, performed better than expected in the World Cup finals of 1990 beating Scotland and Sweden before

65

falling to the Czechs in the second round. Their qualification for 2002 has been spectacular, they only dropped seven points, finished top of their group and in the process beat Mexico at home taking their long standing unbeaten home record. The veteran, Hernan Medford (34) will no doubt hold the Ticos together; his experience and ability to score goals has given him cult status in Costa Rica. Other players to look out for include Paulo Wanchope, Rolando Fonseca and Reynaldo Parks. Costa Rica face China in their first match, a team managed by Bora Milutinovic who was the Ticos manager of 1990. Brazil on the 13th June may not be so closely matched but the Costa Ricans with odds of 200/1 specialise in surprises.

Croatia

Capital City: Zagreb

Location: Part of the Former Yugoslavia, Croatia is a central European nation bordered by Bosnia in the East, Slovenia and Hungary to the North and Yugoslavia to the North East

Land Mass: 56,540 Km Sq

Average monthly income US Dollars: $377 Per Month

Currency: 1 Kuna = 100 Lipa

Population: 4.5 Million

Football in Croatia:

Year Football Federation was founded: 1912

Number of registered football clubs: 1,221

Number of registered players: 78,127

Official website address: www.hns-cff.hr

National colours: Red/white shirts, blue shorts, white socks

67

Previous World Cup Finals Experience:

Previous World Cup finals appearances: 1998

Best position in the finals: Third 1998

Largest victory in the finals: 3-0 V Germany, 1998

Heaviest defeat in the finals: 1-2 V France, 1998

Highest attendance in the finals: 76,000 V France, 1998

Lowest attendance in the finals: 34,700 V Romania, 1998

How Croatia qualified for the World Cup Finals:

How did the qualification process work in Croatia's continent?

51 European Countries entered the qualifications; France were given an automatic qualification place for winning the 1998 World Cup and the remaining 50 teams were split into 4 groups of 5 teams and 5 groups of 6 teams. The group winners were all awarded automatic qualification with the 9 Runners up playing one another with the exception of 1 team (Ireland) who played the winning Runner up of the Asian qualification group (Iran).

Final Position in their group table:

Country	Pl	W	D	L	F	A	GD	Pts
Croatia	*8*	*5*	*3*	*0*	*15*	*2*	*13*	*18*
Belgium	8	5	2	1	25	6	19	17
Scotland	8	4	3	1	12	6	6	15
Latvia	8	1	1	6	5	16	-11	4
San Marino	8	0	1	7	3	30	-27	1

The 2002 Croatia World Cup Team:

Name of the Coach: Mirko Jozic

World ranking (January 2002): 19

Approximate betting odds: 66/1

Drawn in Group: G

Country where they will play the group matches: Japan

Players to watch: Alen Boksic, Bosko Balban, Davor Suker

Overview of Croatia:

Croatia provided the biggest surprise of the 1998 World Cup. Relative newcomers to the international stage, they finished third in the competition demolishing Germany 3-0 in the quarter finals before succumbing to eventual winners France in the semi's. Success has been hard to find since. Having failed to qualify for the European Championships of 2000, the somewhat ageing team needed the introduction of Mirko Jozic as coach to resurrect and restructure a team that looked strong on paper but was riddled with inconsistency. Eventually finishing top of their qualification group, Croatia have been drawn against Italy amongst others in what is hoped to be one of the games of the first round. Young gun Bosko Balban will be one to watch, and it will be interesting to see which of the old guard Jozic decides to give a run out to.

Denmark

Capital City:
Copenhagen

Location: Scandinavian country consisting of most of the Jutland Peninsula, several islands in the Baltic sea and some of the North Fresian island in the North Sea

Land Mass: 43,076 Km Sq

Average monthly income US Dollars: $2,670 Per Month

Currency: 1 Krone = 100 Ore

Population: 5.2 Million

Football in Denmark:

Year Football Federation was founded: 1889

Number of registered football clubs: 1,555

Number of registered players: 268,517

Official website address: www.dbu.dk

National colours: Red shirts, white shorts and red socks

71

Previous World Cup Finals Experience:

Previous World Cup finals appearances: 1986, 1998

Best position in the finals: Quarter Finals, 1998

Largest victory in the finals: 6-1 V Uruguay, 1986

Heaviest defeat in the finals: 1-5 V Spain, 1986

Highest attendance in the finals: 80,000 V Nigeria, 1998

Lowest attendance in the finals: 18,000 V Scotland, 1986

How Denmark qualified for the World Cup Finals:

How did the qualification process work in Denmark's continent?

51 European Countries entered the qualifications; France were given an automatic qualification place for winning the 1998 World Cup and the remaining 50 teams were split into 4 groups of 5 teams and 5 groups of 6 teams. The group winners were all awarded automatic qualification with the 9 Runners up playing one another with the exception of 1 team (Ireland) who played the winning Runner up of the Asian qualification group (Iran).

72

Final Position in their group table:

Country	Pl	W	D	L	F	A	GD	Pts
Denmark	*10*	*6*	*4*	*0*	*22*	*6*	*16*	*22*
Czech Republic	10	6	2	2	20	8	12	20
Bulgaria	10	5	2	3	14	15	-1	17
Iceland	10	4	1	5	14	20	-6	13
Northern Ireland	10	3	2	5	11	12	-1	11

The 2002 Denmark World Cup Team:

Name of the Coach: Morten Olsen

World ranking (January 2002): 17

Approximate betting odds: 125/1

Drawn in Group: A

Country where they will play the group matches: South Korea

Players to watch: Martin Jorgensen, Thomas Helveg, Ebbe Sand

Overview of Denmark:

Four years after their creditable quarter final appearance in France 98, Denmark have witnessed a spectacular fall and recent rise in form.

Finishing bottom of their group in the last European Championships, failing to win a point or score a goal, they have re-established themselves as a winning team by topping their World Cup qualifying group ahead of the Czechs. Up front the Danes boast Ebbe Sand - the Bundesliga's top scorer in the 2000/2001 campaign, with Helveg and Jorgensen both serie A players in Midfield. It will be strange not seeing Peter Schmeichel in goal who after 129 caps has hung up his gloves. His replacement Thomas Sorensen may have his work cut out as Denmark play France on 11th June. Ranked 17th in the world with odds of 125/1- Denmark may yet surprise as they have done before by being recalled from holiday to replace Yugoslavia, and winning the European Championships in 1992.

Ecuador

Capital City: Quinto

Location: Located in the North West of the South American continent, Equador is bordered to the North by Colombia and to the South by Peru

Land Mass: 270,699 Km Sq

Average monthly income US Dollars: $113 Per Month

Currency: 1 US Dollar = 100 Cents

Population: 13 Million

Football in Ecuador:

Year Football Federation was founded: 1925

Number of registered football clubs: 170

Number of registered players: 15,700

Official website address: www.ecuafutbolonline.org

National colours: Yellow shirts with blue and red fringes, blue shorts and red socks

Previous World Cup Finals Experience:

Previous World Cup finals appearances:

Ecuador appear in the World Cup finals for the first time

How Ecuador qualified for the World Cup Finals:

How did the qualification process work in Ecuador's continent?

10 South American countries applied for qualification and played each other at Home and Away on a league basis. The first 4 countries gained automatic qualification with the fifth placed team playing the winner of the Oceania group at Home and Away (Uruguay V Australia).

Final Position in their group table:

Country	Pl	W	D	L	F	A	GD	Pts
Argentina	18	13	4	1	42	15	27	43
Ecuador	*18*	*9*	*4*	*5*	*23*	*20*	*3*	*31*
Brazil	18	9	3	6	31	17	14	30
Paraguay	18	9	3	6	29	23	6	30
Uruguay	18	7	6	5	19	13	6	27
Colombia	18	7	6	5	20	15	5	27
Bolivia	18	4	6	8	21	33	-12	18
Peru	18	4	4	10	14	25	-11	16
Venezuela	18	5	1	12	18	44	-26	16
Chile	18	3	3	12	15	27	-12	12

The 2002 Ecuador World Cup Team:

Name of the Coach: Hernan Dario Gomez

World ranking (January 2002): 37

Approximate betting odds: 100/1

Drawn in Group: G

Country where they will play the group matches: Japan

Players to watch: Agustin Delagado, Ivan Kaviedes, Cevallos

Overview of Ecuador:

Ecuador are one of only four teams to qualify for the finals for the first time in their history. To qualify is a feat in itself, but it is the way that the Ecuadorians did it that has sent shock waves across the globe. During qualification, they managed to pick up 31 points, finish second in their group, beat Brazil and draw with Argentina on the way. Much is down to ex Columbian national coach Gomez, who has a particular way of playing and hates to take chances. He will not be taking Ecuador to Japan to make up numbers though. He is keen to compete and set them firmly on the map in South America where they have been 'also rans' for far too long. Ecuador kick off their campaign against three time champions Italy. A tough start but one where players Delagado, Kaviedes and Cevallos will be hoping to make the right first impression for the debutantes.

77

England

Capital City: London

Location: Largest area within the United Kingdom, an island nation located off the Coast of North West Europe

Land Mass: 130,357 Km Sq

Average monthly income US Dollars: $1,965 Per Month

Currency: 1 Pound Sterling = 100 Pence

Population: 49 Million

Football in England:

Year Football Federation was founded: 1863

Number of registered football clubs: 42,000

Number of registered players: 2.25 Million

Official website address: www.the-fa.org

National colours: White shirt, navy blue shorts and white socks

Previous World Cup Finals Experience:

Previous World Cup finals appearances: 1950, 1954, 1958, 1962, 1966 (Hosts), 1970, 1982, 1986, 1990, 1998

Best position in the finals: Winners, 1966

Largest victory in the finals: 4-2 V West Germany, 1966

Heaviest defeat in the finals: 2-4 V Uruguay, 1954

Highest attendance in the finals: 114,500 V Argentina, 1986

Lowest attendance in the finals: 5,700 V Bulgaria, 1962

How England qualified for the World Cup Finals:

How did the qualification process work in England's continent?

51 European Countries entered the qualifications; France were given an automatic qualification place for winning the 1998 World Cup and the remaining 50 teams were split into 4 groups of 5 teams and 5 groups of 6 teams. The group winners were all awarded automatic qualification with the 9 Runners up playing one another with the exception of 1 team (Ireland) who played the winning Runner up of the Asian qualification group (Iran).

79

Final Position in their group table:

Country	Pl	W	D	L	F	A	GD	Pts
England	8	5	2	1	16	6	10	17
Germany	8	5	2	1	14	10	4	17
Finland	8	3	3	2	12	7	5	12
Greece	8	2	1	5	7	17	-10	7
Albania	8	1	0	7	5	14	-9	3

The 2002 England World Cup Team:

Name of the Coach: Sven Goran Eriksson

World ranking (January 2002): 10

Approximate betting odds: 10/1

Drawn in Group: F

Country where they will play the group matches: Japan

Players to watch: David Beckham, Michael Owen, Paul Scholes

Overview of England:

Sven Goran Eriksson's arrival to manage the England team brought them from the brink of obscurity to win their group and in the process sensationally beat Germany 5-1. England, unseeded having failed to qualify in 1994 have been drawn into probably the toughest Group;

Group F along with Argentina, Nigeria and Sweden. David Beckham will have the chance to rest the demons of his dismissal against Argentina in 1998, and the team will need to overcome the duck that is Sweden, England have not beaten them since 1968. With a flowing passing style of football, Michael Owen, David Beckham and Paul Scholes will be the players to watch. Taming the three lions will be a task for any team, and England will need to remove their unpredictable streak to stand a chance of being 'big in Japan'.

France

Capital City: Paris

Location: Situated in Western Europe and bounded South and East by large mountain ranges

Land Mass: 551,000 Km Sq

Average monthly income US Dollars: $2,014 Per Month

Currency: 1 Euro = 100 Cents

Population: 59 Million

Football in France:

Year Football Federation was founded: 1919

Number of registered football clubs: 21,629

Number of registered players: 1,692,205

Official website address: www.fff.fr

National colours: Blue, white and red shirts. Blue shorts and red socks

Previous World Cup Finals Experience:

Previous World Cup finals appearances: 1930, 1934, 1938 (Hosts), 1954, 1958, 1966, 1978, 1982, 1986, 1998 (Hosts)

Best position in the finals: Winners 1998

Largest victory in the finals: 7-3 V Paraguay, 1958

Heaviest defeat in the finals: 2-5 V Brazil, 1958

Highest attendance in the finals: 98,270 V England, 1966

Lowest attendance in the finals: 1,000 V Mexico, 1930

How France qualified for the World Cup Finals:

How did the qualification process work in France's continent?

51 European Countries entered the qualifications; France were given an automatic qualification place for winning the 1998 World Cup and the remaining 50 teams were split into 4 groups of 5 teams and 5 groups of 6 teams. The group winners were all awarded automatic qualification with the 9 Runners up playing one another with the exception of 1 team (Ireland) who played the winning Runner up of the Asian qualification group (Iran)

The 2002 France World Cup Team:

Name of the Coach: Roger Lemerre

World ranking (January 2002): 1

Approximate betting odds: 5/1

Drawn in Group: A

Country where they will play the group matches: South Korea

Players to watch: Zinedine Zidane, Patrick Vieira, Thierry Henry

Overview of France:

World Cup hosts and winners for 1998, European Championship winners for 2000 and most recently winners of the Confederations Cup, the selection nightmare that Roger Lemerre faces is the envy of the world. The selected 22 squad members chosen for their first match against Senegal will look quite different from the team of 98. They will however still be strong at the back (Barthez, Desailly, Lizarazu, Thuram) have Zidane, Petit, Pires and Nantes' new boy Eric Carriere in Midfield, while David Trezeguet and Thierry Henry will be fighting for the front spot. France will be brimming with confidence and will be the team to beat, but history is unfortunately not on their side; European countries have only ever won the World Cup in Europe and there has not been a successful defence of the World Cup for 40 years. Ranked number one in the world by FIFA and with odds of 5-1, it will be a surprise if France are not seen in the Yokohama stadium in late June.

Germany

Capital City: Berlin

Location: Located in Central Europe, Germany is bordered to the North by Denmark, the East by Poland and the Czech Republic, the South by Austria and Switzerland and the West by France, Luxembourg, Liechtenstein and Holland

Land Mass: 357,868 Km Sq

Average monthly income US Dollars: $2,135 Per Month

Currency: 1 Euro = 100 Cents

Population: 82 Million

Football in Germany:

Year Football Federation was founded: 1900

Number of registered football clubs: 26,760

Number of registered players: 5,260,320

Official website address: www.dfb.de

National colours: White shirts, black shorts and white socks

85

Previous World Cup Finals Experience:

Previous World Cup finals appearances: (NOTE - All statistics include Pre war Germany, West Germany and unified Germany) 1934, 1954, 1958, 1962, 1966, 1970, 1974 (Hosts), 1978, 1982, 1986, 1990, 1994, 1998

Best position in the finals: Winners 1954, 1974, 1990

Largest victory in the finals: 6-0 V Mexico, 1978

Heaviest defeat in the finals: 3-8 V Hungary, 1954

Highest attendance in the finals: 114,590 V Argentina, 1986

Lowest attendance in the finals: 3,000 V Sweden, 1934

How Germany qualified for the World Cup Finals:

How did the qualification process work in Germany's continent?

51 European Countries entered the qualifications; France were given an automatic qualification place for winning the 1998 World Cup and the remaining 50 teams were split into 4 groups of 5 teams and 5 groups of 6 teams. The group winners were all awarded automatic qualification with the 9 Runners up playing one another with the exception of 1

team (Ireland) who played the winning Runner
up of the Asian qualification group (Iran).

Final Position in their group table:

Country	Pl	W	D	L	F	A	GD	Pts
England	8	5	2	1	16	6	10	17
Germany	8	5	2	1	14	10	4	17
Finland	8	3	3	2	12	7	5	12
Greece	8	2	1	5	7	17	-10	7
Albania	8	1	0	7	5	14	-9	3

The 2002 Germany World Cup Team:

Name of the Coach: Rudi Voller

World ranking (January 2002): 11

Approximate betting odds: 11/1

Drawn in Group: E

**Country where they will play the group
matches:** Japan

Players to watch: Oliver Kahn, Carsten Jancker,
Mehmet Scholl

Overview of Germany:

Germany have had a turbulent last four years
having exited the European Championships of

2000 in the first round and thanks to England had to qualify for the World Cup finals via the play offs. Inconsistency seems to have been their problem, one minute losing 5-1 at home to England and then sensationally beating the Ukranians 5-2 on aggregate in the play offs. But the draw has been kind to Germany. Group E consists of Ireland, Saudi Arabia and Cameroon and while they are careful not to write any of their opponents off, coach, former striker and national hero Rudi Voller is sure they will at least reach the Second Round. Players to look out for include Goalkeeper of the year Oliver Kahn, Strikers Neuville and Janker and the Midfield sensation Mehmet Scholl. The Germans have won the World Cup three times before and they could very easily be one of the final 4 if not the final 2.

Italy

Capital City: Rome

Location: A Southern European Nation comprising the bootshaped peninsula extending South into the Mediterranean Sea. Bordered by France, Switzerland, Austria and Slovenia

Land Mass: 310,255 Km Sq

Average monthly income US Dollars: $1,680 Per Month

Currency: 1 Euro = 100 Cents

Population: 57.5 Million

Football in Italy:

Year Football Federation was founded: 1898

Number of registered football clubs: 20,961

Number of registered players: 1,420,160

Official website address: www.figc.it

National colours: Blue shirts, white shorts, blue socks

Previous World Cup Finals Experience:

Previous World Cup finals appearances: 1934 (Hosts), 1938, 1950, 1954, 1962, 1966, 1970, 1974, 1978, 1982, 1986, 1990 (Hosts), 1994, 1998

Best position in the finals: Winners 1934, 1938, 1982

Largest victory in the finals: 7-1 V USA, 1934

Heaviest defeat in the finals: 1-4 V Switzerland 1954, V Brazil,1970

Highest attendance in the finals: 107,000 V Brazil, 1970

Lowest attendance in the finals: 9,000 V Israel, 1970

How Italy qualified for the World Cup Finals:

How did the qualification process work in Italy's continent?

51 European Countries entered the qualifications; France were given an automatic qualification place for winning the 1998 World Cup and the remaining 50 teams were split into 4 groups of 5 teams and 5 groups of 6 teams. The group winners were all awarded automatic qualification with the 9 Runners up playing one another with the exception of 1 team (Ireland) who played the winning Runner up of the Asian qualification group (Iran)

Final Position in their group table:

Country	Pl	W	D	L	F	A	GD	Pts
Italy	8	6	2	0	16	3	13	20
Romania	8	5	1	2	10	7	3	16
Georgia	8	3	1	4	12	12	0	10
Hungary	8	2	2	4	14	13	1	8
Lithuania	8	0	2	6	3	20	-17	2

The 2002 Italy World Cup Team:

Name of the Coach: Giovanni Trapattoni
World ranking (January 2002): 6
Approximate betting odds: 5/1
Drawn in Group: G
Country where they will play the group matches: Japan
Players to watch: Francesco Totti, Paolo Maldini, Christian Vieri

Overview of Italy:

The Italians face an enviable dilemma shared by the French...who to play? With a team packed full of talent, Coach Trapattoni will be desperate to find the right combination, quickly. Three times World Cup winners, European Championship 2000 runners up and runners up to Brazil in the World Cup final of 1994, Italy have plenty of experience and form. Paolo Maldini will be leading the Italians from the back and proving that Italy have one of the best defences in the world. They only conceded three goals during qualification. Trapattoni has encouraged his players to do their homework for round one as only a fool would write off Ecuador, Mexico and Croatia without a Herculean fight. Players to look out for are numerous but include: Vieri, Totti, Cannavaro, Nesta, Del Piero and maybe even the legendary Roberto Baggio.

Japan

Capital City: Tokyo

Location: An Island Nation, Japan is located along the Eastern rim of the Asian continent with Korea, Russia and China to it's North and East

Land Mass: 378,000 Km Sq

Average monthly income US Dollars: $2,669 Per Month

Currency: Yen

Population: 126 Million

Football in Japan:

Year Football Federation was founded: 1921

Number of registered football clubs: 13,047

Number of registered players: 358,989

Official website address: www.jfa.or.jp

National colours: Blue and white shirts, white shorts with blue trim and blue socks with white trim

93

Previous World Cup Finals Experience:

Previous World Cup finals appearances: 1998

Best position in the finals: First Round 1998

Largest victory in the finals: Never won a game in the Finals

Heaviest defeat in the finals: 1-2 V Jamaica, 1998

Highest attendance in the finals: 43,500 V Jamaica, 1998

Lowest attendance in the finals: 33,400 V Argentina, 1998

How Japan qualified for the World Cup Finals:

How did the qualification process work in Japan's continent?

39 Countries entered the qualifications (Japan and South Korea were given a bye as host nations) and played Round 1 in a ten league competition with the winners of each league going forward into the second round. The second round consisted of two Leagues of 5 teams with the winners automatically qualifying and the Runners up playing each other (Iran V UAE). The winning Runner up (Iran) then played the European Runner up of Group 2 (Ireland) for the final position.

The 2002 Japan World Cup Team:

Name of the Coach: Philippe Troussier

World ranking (January 2002): 35

Approximate betting odds: 66/1

Drawn in Group: H

Country where they will play the group matches: Japan

Players to watch: Hidetoshi Nakata, Yoshikatsu Kawaguchi, Shinji Ono

Overview of Japan:

The advent of Japan's own professional football league, 'the J League', has transformed a nation who once viewed football with curiosity rather than with the fanaticism it now receives. Qualifying as a host nation and with all the advantages of home support, Japan will leave the starting blocks with their best chance ever of putting their nation on the World footballing map. Winners of the Asian cup in 2000 and runners up in the Confederation cup of 2001, Japan still have to win a game in the finals; a feat they failed to manage in 1998. Coach Troussier will be relying heavily on the inspirational Hidetoshi Nakata and Shinji Ono to deliver what all the Japanese are praying for; a place in the last 16.

Mexico

Capital City: Mexico City

Location: Located within Central America, Mexico shares borders with the USA (to the North), and Guatemala and Belize (to the South East)

Land Mass: 1,978,800 Km Sq

Average monthly income US Dollars: $370 Per Month

Currency: 1 Peso = 100 Centavos

Population: 96 Million

Football in Mexico:

Year Football Federation was founded: 1927

Number of registered football clubs: 77

Number of registered players: 1,402,270

Official website address: None Known

National colours: Green shirts with white collar. White shorts, red and green socks

96

Previous World Cup Finals Experience:

Previous World Cup finals appearances: 1930, 1950, 1954, 1958, 1962, 1966, 1970 (Hosts), 1978, 1986 (Hosts), 1994, 1998

Best position in the finals: Quarter Finals 1986

Largest victory in the finals: 4-0 V El Salvador, 1970

Heaviest defeat in the finals: 0-6 V West Germany, 1978

Highest attendance in the finals: 114,600 V Paraguay, 1986

Lowest attendance in the finals: 500 V Chile, 1930

How Mexico qualified for the World Cup Finals:

How did the qualification process work in Mexico's continent?

The CONCACAF (Confederation of North Central American and Caribbean Association Football) was probably the most complicated and extensive qualification process. There were three qualification stages - the preliminary phase, the Semi finals and the Final qualification stage. The phases were run on a league basis with Costa Rica, Jamaica, Mexico and USA all getting byes from the first stage having qualified for the World Cup finals before. The final group of six played home and away with the top three in the group qualifying.

Final Position in their group table:

Country	Pl	W	D	L	F	A	GD	Pts
Costa Rica	10	7	2	1	17	7	10	23
Mexico	10	5	2	3	16	9	7	17
USA	10	5	2	3	11	8	3	17
Honduras	10	4	2	4	17	17	0	14
Jamaica	10	1	2	7	5	18	-13	5
Trinidad	10	1	2	7	5	18	-13	5

The 2002 Mexico World Cup Team:

Name of the Coach: Javier Aguirre

World ranking (January 2002): 9

Approximate betting odds: 80/1

Drawn in Group: G

Country where they will play the group matches: Japan

Players to watch: Cuauhtemoc Blanco, Rafel Marquez, Claudio Suarez

Overview of Mexico:

Coach Javier Aguirre ensured Mexico's qualification for the World Cup with an emphatic 3-0 win over Honduras in November 2001. But the road to the finals has been far from easy for the

Mexicans. Aguirre is their third Manager in two years having been bought in to try and resurrect a team who had lost three times in their first five qualification matches. One thing Mexico do have a lot of is World Cup finals experience. Qualifying for the twelfth time, they will be trying to beat their best ever performance when they appeared in the last 8 in their homeland in 1986. Watch out for Cuauhtemoc Blanco and sweeper Claudio Suarez, they will be doing everything they can to beat the much favoured Italians and Croatians. One thing that is certain is that Group G will be a very interesting group to watch as it develops.

Nigeria

Capital City: Abuja

Location: Nigeria is located in Central Western Africa. It sits on the Gulf of Guinea bordered to the North by Niger, the East by Cameroon and the West by Benin

Land Mass: 923,768 Km Sq

Average monthly income US Dollars: $21 Per Month

Currency: 1 Nigerian Naira = 100 Kobo

Population: 115 Million

Football in Nigeria:

Year Football Federation was founded: 1945

Number of registered football clubs: 326

Number of registered players: 80,190

Official website address: www.nfaonline.com

National colours: Green shirts, white shorts and green socks

Previous World Cup Finals Experience:

Previous World Cup finals appearances: 1994, 1998

Best position in the finals: Second Round 1994, 1998

Largest victory in the finals: 3-0 V Bulgaria, 1994

Heaviest defeat in the finals: 1-4 V Denmark, 1998

Highest attendance in the finals: 80,000 V Denmark, 1998

Lowest attendance in the finals: 33,257 V Spain, 1994

How Nigeria qualified for the World Cup Finals:

How did the qualification process work in Nigeria's continent?

50 African teams signed up for the World Cup qualification and 5 places were allocated. 2 Rounds of games were played with Round 1 being a two leg competition (Home and Away) between two countries. The Aggregate winners of Round 1 were then entered into the second Round. The second Round was a simple 5 group league system with the group leaders after eight games qualifying.

Final Position in their group table:

Country	Pl	W	D	L	F	A	GD	Pts
Nigeria	8	5	1	2	15	3	12	16
Liberia	8	5	0	3	10	8	2	15
Sudan	8	4	0	4	8	10	-2	12
Ghana	8	3	2	3	10	9	1	11
Sierra Leone	8	1	1	6	2	15	-13	4

The 2002 Nigeria World Cup Team:

Name of the Coach: Festus Onigbinde

World ranking (January 2002): 40

Approximate betting odds: 50/1

Drawn in Group: F

Country where they will play the group matches: Japan

Players to watch: Augustine Okocha, Nwankwo Kanu, Celestine Babayaro

Overview of Nigeria:

The Super Eagles have appeared in the last two World Cup finals and both times have reached the last 16. They won the African Nations cup in 1994 and the Olympic gold medal in 1996, one thing they don't lack is experience. Blessed with a hugely talented line up, Nigeria have a vast number of players to choose from and maybe this has been half of their problem. On their day Nigeria are as good as anyone in the World, but they are dogged by inconsistency and their qualification matches play testament to this. Nwankwo Kanu, the inspirational Jay Jay Okocha and the solid defender Babyaro are all players to look out for as Nigeria take stage in what has been deemed as the 'group of death'. Not the bookmakers favourite, do not be surprised if they cause the odd upset!

Paraguay

Capital City: Asuncion

Location: A landlocked country located in South America, bordered by Brazil, Bolivia and Argentina

Land Mass: 406,750 Km Sq

Average monthly income US Dollars: $130 Per Month

Currency: 1 Guarani = 100 Centimos

Population: 5.5 Million

Football in Paraguay:

Year Football Federation was founded: 1906

Number of registered football clubs: 1,500

Number of registered players: 140,000

Official website address: None Known

National colours: Red and white shirts, blue shorts and blue socks

Previous World Cup Finals Experience:

Previous World Cup finals appearances: 1930, 1950, 1958, 1986, 1998

Best position in the finals: Second Round 1986, 1998

Largest victory in the finals: 3-1 V Nigeria, 1998

Heaviest defeat in the finals: 3-7 V France, 1958

Highest attendance in the finals: 114,600 V Mexico, 1986

Lowest attendance in the finals: 800 V USA, 1930

How Paraguay qualified for the World Cup Finals:

How did the qualification process work in Paraguay's continent?

10 South American countries applied for qualification and played each other at Home and Away on a league basis. The first 4 countries gained automatic qualification with the fifth placed team playing the winner of the Oceania group at Home and Away (Uruguay V Australia).

Final Position in their group table:

Country	Pl	W	D	L	F	A	GD	Pts
Argentina	18	13	4	1	42	15	27	43
Ecuador	18	9	4	5	23	20	3	31
Brazil	18	9	3	6	31	17	14	30
Paraguay	*18*	*9*	*3*	*6*	*29*	*23*	*6*	*30*
Uruguay	18	7	6	5	19	13	6	27
Colombia	18	7	6	5	20	15	5	27
Bolivia	18	4	6	8	21	33	-12	18
Peru	18	4	4	10	14	25	-11	16
Venezuela	18	5	1	12	18	44	-26	16
Chile	18	3	3	12	15	27	-12	12

The 2002 Paraguay World Cup Team:

Name of the Coach: Cesare Maldini

World ranking (January 2002): 14

Approximate betting odds: 50/1

Drawn in Group: B

Country where they will play the group matches: South Korea

Players to watch: Roque Santa Cruz, Jose Luis Chilavert, Acuna

Overview of Paraguay:

Paraguay's qualification is best described as
eventful! Their final qualification game against
Columbia saw them lose 4-0 and as a result,
Uruguayan coach Sergio Markarian was given his
marching orders. Replacement coach Maldini is
well aware that much of Paraguay's recent success
is down to Markarian, and their superb performance in the 1998 World Cup is testament to him.
Going out to France in the second round thanks
to a Blanc golden goal was rough justice to a team
that had convincingly beaten Nigeria and drawn
against Spain in the early stages. During the World
Cup finals the player to watch has to be Jose Luis
Chilavert. The eccentric goal keeper who has
scored over fifty goals in his career is renowned
for his free kick and penalty taking ability. But
Paraguay will have to do without him for the first
two games as the result of a ban for an incident
with Brazil's Roberto Carlos in August 2001.
Ranked 14th in the world and with some recent
World Cup experience, Paraguay have a strong
chance of making it through to the second round.

Poland

Capital City: Warsaw

Location: Poland is located in central Europe and is bordered by the Baltic Sea to the North-West, by Germany to the West, the Czech and Slovak Republics to the South and Ukraine, Belarus, Lithuania and Russia to the East

Land Mass: 312,683 Km Sq

Average monthly income US Dollars: $339 Per Month

Currency: 1 Zloty = 100 Grosxy

Population: 39 Million

Football in Poland:

Year Football Federation was founded: 1919

Number of registered football clubs: 5,881

Number of registered players: 317,442

Official website address: www.pzpn.pl

National colours: White shirts, red shorts and white socks

Previous World Cup Finals Experience:

Previous World Cup finals appearances: 1938, 1974, 1978, 1982, 1986

Best position in the finals: Third 1974, 1982

Largest victory in the finals: 7-0 V Haiti, 1974

Heaviest defeat in the finals: 0-4 V Brazil, 1986

Highest attendance in the finals: 79,000 V Brazil, 1974

Lowest attendance in the finals: 15,000 V Tunisia, 1978

How Poland qualified for the World Cup Finals:

How did the qualification process work in Poland's continent?

51 European Countries entered the qualifications; France were given an automatic qualification place for winning the 1998 World Cup and the remaining 50 teams were split into 4 groups of 5 teams and 5 groups of 6 teams. The group winners were all awarded automatic qualification with the 9 Runners up playing one another with the exception of 1 team (Ireland) who played the winning Runner up of the Asian qualification group (Iran).

Final Position in their group table:

Country	Pl	W	D	L	F	A	GD	Pts
Poland	*10*	*6*	*3*	*1*	*21*	*11*	*10*	*21*
Ukraine	10	4	5	1	13	8	5	17
Belarus	10	4	3	3	12	11	1	15
Norway	10	2	4	4	12	14	-2	10
Wales	10	1	6	3	10	12	-2	9
Armenia	10	1	6	3	10	12	-2	9

The 2002 Poland World Cup Team:

Name of the Coach: Wladyslaw Engel

World ranking (January 2002): 33

Approximate betting odds: 66/1

Drawn in Group: D

Country where they will play the group matches: South Korea

Players to watch: Emmanuel Olisadebe, Tomasz Hajto, Jerzy Dudek

Overview of Poland:

Poland have seen a huge turn around in fate of late, which began with the arrival of Coach Wladyslaw Engel. Deemed no hopers and with a terrible string of results, Poland began their qualification with a 3-1 win away at Ukraine in September 2000. Things just got better and better for Poland, they won their group with a four point margin, they beat Norway (much to everyone's surprise) and they also secured the talents of the recently naturalised Nigerian Striker Emmanuel Olisadebe. Panathainaikos striker Olisadebe has scored at the rate of a goal a game during qualification, confirming his status as joint top scorer within the Greek League. Poland are also graced with a superb defence. Between the posts, Liverpool's (English Premiership) acrobatic Jerzy Dudek will be standing his ground and in front of him the Schalke 04 defensive partners Tomasz Waldoch and Tomasz Hhatjo will be working together as they do so well in the Bundesliga. Poland are drawn in a tough group and will have to face an on fire Portugal. But fate may have its say; the last time they met was in 1986 in Mexico and Poland won that encounter 1-0.

Portugal

Capital City: Lisbon

Location: Located on the Western side of the Iberian Peninsula, Portugal is bordered to the North and East by Spain and to the West forms the coastline to the Atlantic Ocean

Land Mass: 91,630 Km Sq

Average monthly income US Dollars: $919 Per Month

Currency: 1 Euro = 100 Cents

Population: 10 Million

Football in Portugal:

Year Football Federation was founded: 1914

Number of registered football clubs: 204

Number of registered players: 79,235

Official website address: www.fpf.pt

National colours: Red shirts, green shorts and red socks

Previous World Cup Finals Experience:

Previous World Cup finals appearances: 1966, 1986

Best position in the finals: Third 1966

Largest victory in the finals: 3-0 V Bulgaria, 1966

Heaviest defeat in the finals: 1-3 V Morroco, 1986

Highest attendance in the finals: 94,493 V England, 1966

Lowest attendance in the finals: 19,915 V Poland, 1986

How Portugal qualified for the World Cup Finals:

How did the qualification process work in Portugal's continent?

51 European Countries entered the qualifications; France were given an automatic qualification place for winning the 1998 World Cup and the remaining 50 teams were split into 4 groups of 5 teams and 5 groups of 6 teams. The group winners were all awarded automatic qualification with the 9 Runners up playing one another with the exception of 1 team (Ireland) who played the winning Runner up of the Asian qualification group (Iran).

Final Position in their group table:

Country	Pl	W	D	L	F	A	GD	Pts
Portugal	*10*	*7*	*3*	*0*	*33*	*7*	*24*	*24*
Ireland	10	7	3	0	23	5	18	24
Holland	10	6	2	2	30	9	21	20
Estonia	10	2	2	6	10	26	-16	8
Cyprus	10	2	2	6	13	31	-18	8

The 2002 Portugal World Cup Team:

Name of the Coach: Antonio Oliveira

World ranking (January 2002): 4

Approximate betting odds: 11/1

Drawn in Group: D

Country where they will play the group matches: South Korea

Players to watch: Luis Figo, Rui Costa, Paulo Sousa

Overview of Portugal:

Ranked fourth in the world and heavily backed by the bookmakers, it would seem that the Portuguese 'golden generation' have one last chance to win World Cup glory. Their recent success in the European Championships in 2000 as semi finalists gave them the boost they needed having failed to qualify for the World Cup in 1998. The Portuguese are renowned for their beautiful

114

flowing football so much so that their local media
have deemed it too beautiful and not workman like
enough. Luis Figo was voted world player of the
year 2001, and he will no doubt be one of the
sensations of the tournament. Players to also
watch out for include Costa, Sousa and Pinto.
Drawn with South Korea, the USA and Poland,
Portugal are group favourites and it will be a
surprise if they do not make it to at least the last 8.

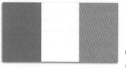

Republic of Ireland

Capital City: Dublin

Location: Western European Island located off the West coast of the United Kingdom and bordered to the North by Northern Ireland

Land Mass: 70,282 Km Sq

Average monthly income US Dollars: $1,789 Per Month

Currency: 1 Euro = 100 Cents

Population: 3.7 Million

Football in The Republic of Ireland:

Year Football Federation was founded: 1921

Number of registered football clubs: 3,190

Number of registered players: 124,615

Official website address: www.fai.ie

National colours: Green shirts, white shorts, green and white socks

116

Previous World Cup Finals Experience:

Previous World Cup finals appearances: 1990, 1994

Best position in the finals: Quarter Finals 1990

Largest victory in the finals: 1-0 V Italy, 1994

Heaviest defeat in the finals: 0-2 V Holland, 1994

Highest attendance in the finals: 76,332 V Norway, 1994

Lowest attendance in the finals: 31,818 V Romania, 1990

How The Republic of Ireland qualified for the World Cup Finals:

How did the qualification process work in Republic of Ireland's continent?

51 European Countries entered the qualifications; France were given an automatic qualification place for winning the 1998 World Cup and the remaining 50 teams were split into 4 groups of 5 teams and 5 groups of 6 teams. The group winners were all awarded automatic qualification with the 9 Runners up playing one another with the exception of 1 team (Ireland) who played the winning Runner up of the Asian qualification group (Iran).

Final Position in their group table:

Country	Pl	W	D	L	F	A	GD	Pts
Portugal	10	7	3	0	33	7	24	24
Ireland	*10*	*7*	*3*	*0*	*23*	*5*	*18*	*24*
Holland	10	6	2	2	30	9	21	20
Estonia	10	2	2	6	10	26	-16	8
Cyprus	10	2	2	6	13	31	-18	8

The 2002 Republic of Ireland World Cup Team:

Name of the Coach: Mick McCarthy

World ranking (January 2002): 18

Approximate betting odds: 66/1

Drawn in Group: E

Country where they will play the group matches: Japan

Players to watch: Roy Keane, Damien Duff, Robbie Keane

Overview of Republic of Ireland:

Qualification was deemed a miracle for the Republic of Ireland. On their way to Japan, they had to match an 'on fire' Portugal, beat favourites Holland and travel to Tehran in the payoffs while holding on to a two goal advantage against the Iranians. They succeeded in all of these challenges and Mick McCarthy's boys go to the World Cup finals for the third time. Jack Charlton managed the last 16 in 1994 and the quarter finals in 1990. There is no doubt the Irish will be out to match or better that record. Qualification and their turn in form can be put down to a number of factors, but there is no doubt that the appointment of Roy Keane as Captain was an inspired choice. Players to watch out for include Duff, both Robbie and Roy Keane (no relation), Charlton's (English Premiership) Mark Kinsella and Fulham's (English Premiership) Steve Finnan. Win, lose or draw, the Irish fans will enjoy every minute of it and will be trying as hard to get behind their team as they did in 1994.

Russia

Capital City: Moscow

Location: Russia occupies most of Eastern Europe and Northern Asia

Land Mass: 17,075,044 Km Sq

Average monthly income US Dollars: $187 Per Month

Currency: 1 Rouble = 100 Kopecs

Population: 148 Million

Football in Russia:

Year Football Federation was founded: 1912

Number of registered football clubs: 43,700

Number of registered players: 785,000

Official website address: ww.rfs.ru

National colours: White and light blue shirts. White shorts and white socks

120

Previous World Cup Finals Experience:

Previous World Cup finals appearances: 1958, 1962, 1966, 1970, 1982, 1986, 1990, 1994

Best position in the finals: Fourth 1966

Largest victory in the finals: 6-0 V Hungary, 1986

Heaviest defeat in the finals: 1-3 V Sweden, 1994

Highest attendance in the finals: 107,000 V Brazil, 1970

Lowest attendance in the finals: 8,040 V Colombia, 1962

How Russia qualified for the World Cup Finals:

How did the qualification process work in Russia's continent?

51 European Countries entered the qualifications; France were given an automatic qualification place for winning the 1998 World Cup and the remaining 50 teams were split into 4 groups of 5 teams and 5 groups of 6 teams. The group winners were all awarded automatic qualification with the 9 Runners up playing one another with the exception of 1 team (Ireland) who played the winning Runner up of the Asian qualification group (Iran).

Final Position in their group table:

Country	Pl	W	D	L	F	A	GD	Pts
Russia	*10*	*7*	*2*	*1*	*18*	*5*	*13*	*23*
Slovenia	10	5	5	0	17	9	8	20
Yugoslavia	10	5	4	1	22	8	14	19
Swiss	10	4	2	4	18	12	6	14
Faroe Islands	10	2	1	7	6	23	-17	7

The 2002 Russia World Cup Team:

Name of the Coach: Oleg Romantsev

World ranking (January 2002): 22

Approximate betting odds: 50/1

Drawn in Group: H

Country where they will play the group matches: Japan

Players to watch: Viktor Onopko, Vladimir Beschastnykh, Alexandre Mostovoi

Overview of Russia:

Russian national Coach Oleg Romanstev is unusually also the coach of Russian league Champions Spartak Moscow. Unsurprisingly, his choice of team is often modeled on his Champions league squad, but with the success Romanstev has

122

brought to the national side few are complaining. Russia failed to qualify for the 1998 World Cup and European Championships of 2000, and success in Japan is a much needed tonic to a football fanatical nation. Within the qualifying rounds, Russia made light work of their group finishing top and losing only once, away to Slovenia. Veteran defender Viktor Onopko and striker Vladimir Beschatnykh are players to watch in a competition that could easily see Russia qualifying for the last 16 in their very open group.

Saudi Arabia

Capital City: Riyadh

Location: Comprising of 80% of the Arabian peninsula, Saudi Arabia is bordered to the South-East by Oman, Yemen and the United Arab Emirates, to the North by Iraq and Kuwait, and to the West by Jordan

Land Mass: 2,331,000 Km Sq

Average monthly income US Dollars: $575 Per Month

Currency: 1 Riyal = 100 Halalah

Population: 21 Million

Football in Saudi Arabia:

Year Football Federation was founded: 1959

Number of registered football clubs: 120

Number of registered players: 9,600

Official website address: None Known

National colours: White shirts with green edging. White shorts and white socks

Previous World Cup Finals Experience:

Previous World Cup finals appearances: 1994, 1998

Best position in the finals: Second Round 1994

Largest victory in the finals: 2-1 V Morocco, 1994

Heaviest defeat in the finals: 0-4 V France, 1998

Highest attendance in the finals: 75,000 V France, 1998

Lowest attendance in the finals: 34,500 V South Africa, 1998

How Saudi Arabia qualified for the World Cup Finals:

How did the qualification process work in Saudi Arabia's continent?

39 Countries entered the qualifications (Japan and South Korea were given a bye as host nations) and played Round 1 in a ten league competition with the winners of each league going forward into the second round. The second round consisted of two Leagues of 5 teams with the winners automatically qualifying and the Runners up playing each other (Iran V UAE). The winning Runner up (Iran) then played the European Runner up of Group 2 (Ireland) for the final position.

Final Position in their group table:

Country	Pl	W	D	L	F	A	GD	Pts
Saudi Arabia	*8*	*5*	*2*	*1*	*17*	*8*	*9*	*17*
Iran	8	4	3	1	10	7	3	15
Bahrain	8	2	4	2	8	9	-1	10
Iraq	8	2	1	5	9	10	-1	7
Thailand	8	0	4	4	5	15	-10	4

The 2002 Saudi Arabia World Cup Team:

Name of the Coach: Nasser Al-Johar

World ranking (January 2002): 30

Approximate betting odds: 300/1

Drawn in Group: E

Country where they will play the group matches: Japan

Players to watch: Nawaf Al Temyat, Sami Al Jaber

Overview of Saudi Arabia:

Qualification for Saudi Arabia has been a tough, turbulent time. The appointment of Coach Nasser Al Johar was the catalyst needed to bring in vital points, in a group that was led by Iran right up to the wire. A last match win against Thailand, and a Bahrain win against Iran ensured the Kingdom of Saudi Arabia would appear in the last 32 for

126

the third succesive time. Rated as rank outsiders, their inability to export players has not helped to increase much needed experience outside of their domestic game. Sami Al Jaber and Nawaf Al Temyat are players to look out for. Al Jaber makes his third World Cup appearance, and much is expected of Al Temyat currently the Asian player of the year. Facing Germany in their first match, the Saudi's will need a solid performance to prevent their Arabian nightmare of 1998.

Senegal

Capital City: Dakar

Location: Located in Western Africa in the Western most part of the "bulge of Africa". Senegal totally surrounds the small nation The Gambia

Land Mass: 196,790 Km Sq

Average monthly income US Dollars: $41.50 Per Month

Currency: 1CFA Franc = 100 Centimes

Population: 10 Million

Football in Senegal:

Year Football Federation was founded: 1960

Number of registered football clubs: 75

Number of registered players: 3,977

Official website address: None Known

National colours: White shirts with green, yellow and red trim. White shorts and white socks

Previous World Cup Finals Experience:

Previous World Cup finals appearances:
Senegal appear in the World Cup finals for the first time.

How Senegal qualified for the World Cup Finals:

How did the qualification process work in Senegal's continent?

50 African teams signed up for the World Cup qualification and 5 places were allocated. 2 Rounds of games were played with Round 1 being a two leg competition (Home and Away) between two countries. The Aggregate winners of Round 1 were then entered into the second Round. The second Round was a simple 5 group league system with the group leaders after eight games qualifying.

Final Position in their group table:

Country	Pl	W	D	L	F	A	GD	Pts
Senegal	8	4	3	1	14	2	12	15
Morocco	8	3	4	1	16	7	9	13
Algeria	8	2	2	4	11	14	-3	8
Namibia	8	0	2	6	3	26	-23	2

The 2002 Senegal World Cup Team:

Name of the Coach: Bruno Metsu

World ranking (January 2002): 67

Approximate betting odds: 200/1

Drawn in Group: A

Country where they will play the group matches: South Korea

Players to watch: Elhadji Diouf, Khalilou Fadida, Pape Sarr

Overview of Senegal:

Dubbed the 'African underdogs', the World Cup new boys are the only qualifying African nation with no World Cup finals experience under their belt. Having come so close as 2002 African nations runners up, Senegal will be out to make their mark on the world football map. Qualification sat on a knife edge right up to their final game against Namibia where they won 5-0 and qualified ahead of Morocco on goal difference. With the majority of their players based in France, as a former French colony and with a French coach, it is apt that they open the tournament facing 1998 World Cup winners France, in what is hoped to be gripping game. Having scored nine of Senegal's fourteen goals in their qualification, prolific goal scorer and Lens striker Elhadji Diouf is the player to watch. Senegal are hoping to surprise the world and cause a few upsets in the process, but whatever happens Senegal will be playing without pressure especially at the opening match on 31st May.

Slovenia

Capital City: Ljubljana

Location: Part of the Former Republic of Yugoslavia. Located between Austria and Croatia

Land Mass: 20,251 Km Sq

Average monthly income US Dollars: $833 Per Month

Currency: 1 Tolar = 100 Stotin

Population: 2 Million

Football in Slovenia:

Year Football Federation was founded: 1920

Number of registered football clubs: 375

Number of registered players: 20,117

Official website address: www.nzs.si

National colours: White shirts, green shorts and white socks

Previous World Cup Finals Experience:

Previous World Cup finals appearances:
Slovenia appear in the World Cup finals for the first time

How Slovenia qualified for the World Cup Finals:

How did the qualification process work in Slovenia's continent?

51 European Countries entered the qualifications; France were given an automatic qualification place for winning the 1998 World Cup and the remaining 50 teams were split into 4 groups of 5 teams and 5 groups of 6 teams. The group winners were all awarded automatic qualification with the 9 Runners up playing one another with the exception of 1 team (Ireland) who played the winning Runner up of the Asian qualification group (Iran).

Final Position in their group table:

Country	Pl	W	D	L	F	A	GD	Pts
Russia	10	7	2	1	18	5	13	23
Slovenia	*10*	*5*	*5*	*0*	*17*	*9*	*8*	*20*
Yugoslavia	10	5	4	1	22	8	14	19
Switzerland	10	4	2	4	18	12	6	14
Faroe Islands	10	2	1	7	6	23	-17	7

The 2002 Slovenia World Cup Team:

Name of the Coach: Srecko Katanec

World ranking (January 2002): 27

Approximate betting odds: 150/1

Drawn in Group: B

Country where they will play the group matches: South Korea

Players to watch: Zlatko Zahovic, Amir Karic, Miran Pavlin

Overview of Slovenia:

With only 2 Million inhabitants, Slovenia are the smallest country to qualify for the World Cup finals. Since 1991 and their break away from Yugoslavia, their football has got progressively better. They managed to qualify for the European championships of 2000 and although finishing fourth in their group, achieved two respectable draws and in the process gained valuable experience. Zlatko Zahovic is the man to watch. The inspirational player scored 29 goals in his first 58 appearances and as a result is the linch pin within the Slovenian team. Zahovic is also quite temperamental and he will need to keep a lid on his emotions if Slovenia are to qualify for the second stage. Ranked 27th in the world and with odds against them in the hundreds, Slovenia will just be pleased to be in South Korea where their former masters Yugoslavia are not. A draw on the 5th September ensured the Yugoslavians finished third and out of the finals....apparently the Slovenians are still celebrating !

South Africa

Capital City: Pretoria

Location: Located on the Southern cusp of Africa. Bordered by Namibia, Botswana, Zimbabwe, Mozambique, Swaziland and surrounds Lesotho

Land Mass: 1,233,404 Km Sq

Average monthly income US Dollars: $264 Per Month

Currency: 1 Rand = 100 Cents

Population: 44 Million

Football in South Africa:

Year Football Federation was founded: 1991

Number of registered football clubs: 51,944

Number of registered players: 1,039,880

Official website address: www.safa.org.za

National colours: Gold and black shirts, green shorts and white socks

Previous World Cup Finals Experience:

Previous World Cup finals appearances: 1998

Best position in the finals: First Round 1998

Largest victory in the finals: Never won a game in the Finals

Heaviest defeat in the finals: 0-3 V France, 1998

Highest attendance in the finals: 55,077 V France, 1998

Lowest attendance in the finals: 34,500 V Saudi Arabia, 1998

How South Africa qualified for the World Cup Finals:

How did the qualification process work in South Africa's continent?

50 African teams signed up for the World Cup qualification and 5 places were allocated. 2 Rounds of games were played with Round 1 being a two leg competition (Home and Away) between two countries. The Aggregate winners of Round 1 were then entered into the second Round. The second Round was a simple 5 group league system with the group leaders after eight games qualifying.

Final Position in their group table:

Country	Pl	W	D	L	F	A	GD	Pts
South Africa	6	5	1	0	10	3	7	16
Zimbabwe	6	4	0	2	7	5	2	12
Burkina Faso	6	1	2	3	7	8	-1	5
Malawi	6	0	1	5	4	12	-8	1

The 2002 South Africa World Cup Team:

Name of the Coach: Carlos Queiroz

World ranking (January 2002): 34

Approximate betting odds: 100/1

Drawn in Group: B

Country where they will play the group matches: South Korea

Players to watch: Shaun Bartlett, Delron Buckley, Lucas Radebe

Overview of South Africa:

'Bafana Bafana', translated as 'The Boys, The Boys' as the South African team is known, appear at their second World Cup finals having not yet won a game in the finals competition. Qualification was never in doubt, winning five and drawing one game in a group that included Malawi and Burkina Faso. Captain and star player Shaun Bartlett is the one

to watch. Playing for Charlton Athletic (English
Premiership) his game has come on significantly
in the last three years and he will be a much
needed rudder for a reasonably inexperienced
South African team. South Africa won the 1996
African Nations cup, and having tasted victory
before they are not a country to be ruled out of
reaching the second round.

South Korea

Capital City: Seoul

Location: Occupying the Southern half of the Korean Peninsula. South Korea is bordered to the North by North Korea and is seperated by the demilitarised 38th Parallel.

Land Mass: 98,915 Km Sq

Average monthly income US Dollars: $708 Per Month

Currency: Won

Population: 47 Million

Football in South Korea:

Year Football Federation was founded: 1928

Number of registered football clubs: 476

Number of registered players: 2,047

Official website address: www.kfa.or.kr

National colours: Red shirts, blue shorts and blue socks

138

Previous World Cup Finals Experience:

Previous World Cup finals appearances: 1954, 1986, 1990, 1994, 1998

Best position in the finals: First Round 1954, 1986, 1990, 1994, 1998

Largest victory in the finals: Never won a game in the Finals

Heaviest defeat in the finals: 0-9 V Hungary, 1954

Highest attendance in the finals: 63,998 V Germany, 1994

Lowest attendance in the finals: 4,000 V Turkey, 1954

How South Korea qualified for the World Cup Finals:

How did the qualification process work in South Korea's continent?

39 Countries entered the qualifications (Japan and South Korea were given a bye as host nations) and played Round 1 in a ten league competition with the winners of each league going forward into the second round. The second round consisted of two Leagues of 5 teams with the winners automatically qualifying and the Runners up playing each other (Iran V UAE). The winning Runner up (Iran) then played the European Runner up of Group 2 (Ireland) for the final position.

139

The 2002 South Korea World Cup Team:

Name of the Coach: Guus Hiddink

World ranking (January 2002): 43

Approximate betting odds: 66/1

Drawn in Group: D

Country where they will play the group matches: South Korea

Players to watch: Yoo Sang-Chul, Seol Ki-Hyeon, Hong Myung-bo

Overview of South Korea:

Korea qualify as a host nation and are hoping that they will win a game during the finals, a feat they have not managed in five previous appearances. Dutch coach Hiddink (appointed in 2001) has added the extra dimension that the Korean team has been so lacking of late. They will obviously have a massive local following which will help them, but whether South Korea can cope with the physical side of the game is still to be seen. Seol Ki-Hyeon is the player to watch, the top Anderlecht (Belgian League) striker will score goals if he is given service. South Korea have a tough group and although claiming they will make the second round, they will need to overcome the on form Portugal on the 14th June to stand a chance.

Spain

Capital City: Madrid

Location: Located in South West Europe, occupying 80% of the Iberian Peninsula. Bordered to the East by Portugal and the North by France

Land Mass: 504,750 Km Sq

Average monthly income US Dollars: $1,233 Per Month

Currency: 1 Euro = 100 Cents

Population: 40 Million

Football in Spain:

Year Football Federation was founded: 1913

Number of registered football clubs: 10,240

Number of registered players: 408,135

Official website address: www.futvol.com

National colours: Red shirts, blue shorts and blue socks with red, blue and yellow border

141

Previous World Cup Finals Experience:

Previous World Cup finals appearances: 1934, 1950, 1962, 1966, 1978, 1982 (Hosts), 1986, 1990, 1994, 1998

Best position in the finals: 4th Position, 1950

Largest victory in the finals: 6-1 V Bulgaria, 1998

Heaviest defeat in the finals: 1-6 V Brazil, 1950

Highest attendance in the finals: 152,722 V Brazil, 1950

Lowest attendance in the finals: 9,511 V USA, 1950

How Spain qualified for the World Cup Finals:

How did the qualification process work in Spain's continent?

51 European Countries entered the qualifications; France were given an automatic qualification place for winning the 1998 World Cup and the remaining 50 teams were split into 4 groups of 5 teams and 5 groups of 6 teams. The group winners were all awarded automatic qualification with the 9 Runners up playing one another with the exception of 1 team (Ireland) who played the winning Runner up of the Asian qualification group (Iran).

Final Position in their group table:

Country	Pl	W	D	L	F	A	GD	Pts
Spain	8	6	2	0	21	4	17	20
Austria	8	4	3	1	10	8	2	15
Israel	8	3	3	2	11	7	4	12
Bosnia	8	2	2	4	12	12	0	8
Liechtenstein	8	0	0	8	0	23	-23	0

The 2002 Spain World Cup Team:

Name of the Coach: Jose Antonio Camacho

World ranking (January 2002): 7

Approximate betting odds: 8/1

Drawn in Group: B

Country where they will play the group matches: South Korea

Players to watch: Raul Gonzalez Blanco, Fernando Hierro, Josep Guardiola

Overview of Spain:

Spain travel to South Korea for their eleventh World Cup finals having successfully won one of the easier qualification groups. Spain as always are full of promise. Coach, Jose Comacho who joined the Spanish setup in 1998, has encouraged

143

an attacking game which seems to suit the players, but as ever with the Spanish, consistency is their greatest enemy. With a best ever World Cup finals finish of fourth place in 1950, the Spanish fans are tiring of the lack of overdue success. The draw in Busan could not have been kinder for Spain, they join Group B as the favourites with every chance of qualifying for the second stage. Players to watch include the inspirational Raul and topscoring defender Hierro. Spain are a heavily backed team who have a very good chance of going the whole way, to be successful they will just need to maintain their consistency and have confidence in their style of play.

Sweden

Capital City: Stockholm

Location: A European Country occupying the Eastern side of the Scandinavian Peninsula. Bordered by Denmark to the South, Norway to the East and Finland to the West

Land Mass: 411,479 Km Sq

Average monthly income US Dollars: $2,229 Per Month

Currency: 1 Swedish Krona = 100 Ore

Population: 9 Million

Football in Sweden:

Year Football Federation was founded: 1904

Number of registered football clubs: 3,250

Number of registered players: 485,000

Official website address: www.svenskfotboll.se

National colours: Yellow shirts, blue shorts and yellow socks

145

Previous World Cup Finals Experience:

Previous World Cup finals appearances: 1934, 1938, 1950, 1958 (Hosts), 1970, 1974, 1978, 1990, 1994

Best position in the finals: Second 1958

Largest victory in the finals: 8-0 V Cuba, 1938

Heaviest defeat in the finals: 1-7 V Brazil, 1950

Highest attendance in the finals: 138,885 V Brazil, 1950

Lowest attendance in the finals: 3,000 V Germany, 1934

How Sweden qualified for the World Cup Finals:

How did the qualification process work in Sweden's continent?

51 European Countries entered the qualifications; France were given an automatic qualification place for winning the 1998 World Cup and the remaining 50 teams were split into 4 groups of 5 teams and 5 groups of 6 teams. The group winners were all awarded automatic qualification with the 9 Runners up playing one another with the exception of 1 team (Ireland) who played the winning Runner up of the Asian qualification group (Iran).

Final Position in their group table:

Country	Pl	W	D	L	F	A	GD	Pts
Sweden	10	8	2	0	20	3	17	26
Turkey	10	6	3	1	18	8	10	21
Slovakia	10	5	2	3	16	9	7	17
Macedonia	10	1	4	5	11	18	-7	7
Moldova	10	1	3	6	6	20	-14	6
Azerbaijan	10	1	2	7	4	17	-13	5

The 2002 Sweden World Cup Team:

Name of the Coach: Tommy Soderberg & Lars Lagerback

World ranking (January 2002): 16

Approximate betting odds: 66/1

Drawn in Group: F

Country where they will play the group matches: Japan

Players to watch: Henrik Larsson, Fredrik Ljungberg, Zlatan Ibrahimovic

Overview of Sweden:

'Lucky Sweden' as they were known when the World Cup qualification groups were announced in 2000. The draw was so kind to them that they were expected to be on their way to the finals having hardly broken sweat. After a slightly lacklustre start they did exactly that, winning their last seven games and dropping only four points over 10 matches. The World Cup finals draw though could not have been crueler. Drawn in the same group as England, Argentina and Nigeria, Group F has been appropriately named 'the group of death'. Joint Coaches Soderburg and Lagerback are pleased not to be favorites and have even gone so far as saying it will be 'fun' and a 'spectacle'. One thing that can be said for them is they know their team well and have certainly varied their options. At the last count they had given 61 players a run out in the last 20 games. Players to watch out for include the young Ibrahimovic, the ever improving and on form Ljungberg and of course Celtic's (Scottish Premiership) Henrik Larsson. Larsson was awarded the European golden boot for his tally during the 2000/2001 season and he remains on target, scoring 4 against Maldova in June 2001.

Tunisia

Capital City: Tunis

Location: Tunisia is a North African nation wedged between Libya and Algeria to the East and West, with the Mediterranean Sea to the North

Land Mass: 163, 610 Km Sq

Average monthly income US Dollars: $174 Per Month

Currency: 1 Tunisian Dinar = 1,000 Millimes

Population: 9 Million

Football in Tunisia:

Year Football Federation was founded: 1956

Number of registered football clubs: 215

Number of registered players: 18,300

Official website address: www.ftf.com.tn

National colours: White shirts with red trim. White shorts. White socks with red tops

149

Previous World Cup Finals Experience:

Previous World Cup finals appearances: 1978, 1998

Best position in the finals: First Round

Largest victory in the finals: 3-1 V Mexico, 1978

Heaviest defeat in the finals: 0-2 V England, 1998

Highest attendance in the finals: 80,000 V Romania, 1998

Lowest attendance in the finals: 15,000 V Poland, 1978

How Tunisia qualified for the World Cup Finals:

How did the qualification process work in Tunisia's continent?

50 African teams signed up for the World Cup qualification and 5 places were allocated. 2 rounds of games were played with Round 1 being a two leg competition between a seeded and non seeded nation. The Aggregate winners of Round 1 were then entered into five, 5 team groups and the winners after 8 games qualified.

Final Position in their group table:

Country	Pl	W	D	L	F	A	GD	Pts
Tunisia	8	6	2	0	23	4	19	20
Ivory Coast	8	4	3	1	18	8	10	15
Congo DR	8	3	1	4	7	16	-9	10
Madagascar	8	2	0	6	5	15	-10	6
Congo	8	1	2	5	5	15	-10	5

The 2002 Tunisia World Cup Team:

Name of the Coach: Henri Michel

World ranking (January 2002): 28

Approximate betting odds: 250/1

Drawn in Group: H

Country where they will play the group matches: Japan

Players to watch: Chokri El Ouaer, Hassen Gabsi, Adel Sellimi

Overview of Tunisia:

On the 2nd June 1978, Tunisia made World Cup history. In their first finals game, they became the first African nation to win a match beating Mexico 3-1. Tunisia have not won a game in the World Cup finals since that day despite qualifying again four years ago in France. A semi final appearance in the 1996 African Nations cup was Tunisia's last triumph, but that is not to say that they will not be a team to watch out for. Their squad of 1998 has few changes and this experience will only benefit a team desperate to make it into the last 16. Adel Sellimi and Goalkeeper Captain Chokri El Ouaer are players to watch. Sellimi of Freiburg (German Bundesliga) has found his form after a poor start at his German club and is now a prolific striker. Pooled in Group H with Japan, Russia and Belgium, the Tunisians along with the critics believe that anything could happen in what is being described as one of the more open groups.

Turkey

Capital City: Ankara

Location: Straddling the continents of Europe and Asia, Turkey provides coastline to the Black Sea in the North and the Mediterranean sea in the South

Land Mass: 799,452 Km Sq

Average monthly income US Dollars: $241 Per Month

Currency: Turkish Lira

Population: 66 Million

Football in Turkey

Year Football Federation was founded: 1923

Number of registered football clubs: 230

Number of registered players: 64,521

Official website address: www.tff.org

National colours: Red and white shirts, shorts and socks

153

Previous World Cup Finals Experience:

Previous World Cup finals appearances: 1954

Best position in the finals: First Round 1954

Largest victory in the finals: 7-0 V South Korea, 1954

Heaviest defeat in the finals: 2-7 V West Germany, 1954

Highest attendance in the finals: 28,000 V West Germany, 1954

Lowest attendance in the finals: 4,000 V South Korea, 1954

How Turkey qualified for the World Cup Finals:

How did the qualification process work in Turkey's continent?

51 European Countries entered the qualifications; France were given an automatic qualification place for winning the 1998 World Cup and the remaining 50 teams were split into 4 groups of 5 teams and 5 groups of 6 teams. The group winners were all awarded automatic qualification with the 9 Runners up playing one another with the exception of 1 team (Ireland) who played the winning Runner up of the Asian qualification group (Iran).

Final Position in their group table:

Country	Pl	W	D	L	F	A	GD	Pts
Sweden	10	8	2	0	20	3	17	26
Turkey	10	6	3	1	18	8	10	21
Slovakia	10	5	2	3	16	9	7	17
Macedonia	10	1	4	5	11	18	-7	7
Moldova	10	1	3	6	6	20	-14	6
Azerbaijan	10	1	2	7	4	17	-13	5

The 2002 Turkey World Cup Team:

Name of the Coach: Senol Gunes

World ranking (January 2002): 23

Approximate betting odds: 100/1

Drawn in Group: C

Country where they will play the group matches: South Korea

Players to watch: Hakan Sukur, Alpay Ozalan, Kerimoglu Tugay

Overview of Turkey:

Newly appointed coach Gunes has survived the barrage of criticism from the Turkish media, proving them all wrong and leading Turkey to the World Cup finals for their second time. Arriving via the

155

play offs, an 'on fire' Turkey beat Austria 6-0 on aggregate confirming their first appearance for nearly 50 years. Facing Brazil in their first game, the Turks claim not to be afraid. They produced a solid performance in the European Championships of 2000 departing in the quarter finals to Portugal, and with a number of their players gaining European exposure within the domestic league, they now have more experience to fall back upon. Hakan Sukur, Inter Milan's striker is a player to watch along with the talented goalkeeper Recber and winger Tugay. Turkey are convinced they will emerge from the group for the last 16 but Brazil may have something to say about that!

Uruguay

Capital City: Montevideo

Location: Located on the East coast of South America and bordered by Brazil and Argentina. Uruguay is cut in half by the Negro river

Land Mass: 176,215 Km Sq

Average monthly income US Dollars: $518 Per Month

Currency: 1 Uruguayan Peso = 100 Centesimos

Population: 3.2 Million

Football in Uruguay:

Year Football Federation was founded: 1900

Number of registered football clubs: 1,091

Number of registered players: 134,310

Official website address: www.auf.org.uy

National colours: Sky blue shirts with white collars and cuffs. Black shorts, black socks with sky blue edges

157

Previous World Cup Finals Experience:

Previous World Cup finals appearances: 1930 (Hosts), 1950, 1954, 1962, 1966, 1970, 1974, 1986, 1990

Best position in the finals: Winners 1930, 1950

Largest victory in the finals: 8-1 V Bolivia, 1950

Heaviest defeat in the finals: 1-6 V Denmark, 1986

Highest attendance in the finals: 199,850 V Brazil, 1950

Lowest attendance in the finals: 5,285 V Bolivia, 1950

How Uruguay qualified for the World Cup Finals:

How did the qualification process work in Uruguay's continent?

10 South American countries applied for qualification and played each other at Home and Away on a league basis. The first 4 countries gained automatic qualification with the fifth placed team playing the winner of the Oceania group at Home and Away (Uruguay V Australia).

Final Position in their group table:

Country	Pl	W	D	L	F	A	GD	Pts
Argentina	18	13	4	1	42	15	27	43
Ecuador	18	9	4	5	23	20	3	31
Brazil	18	9	3	6	31	17	14	30
Paraguay	18	9	3	6	29	23	6	30
Uruguay	18	7	6	5	19	13	6	27
Colombia	18	7	6	5	20	15	5	27
Bolivia	18	4	6	8	21	33	-12	18
Peru	18	4	4	10	14	25	-11	16
Venezuela	18	5	1	12	18	44	-26	16
Chile	18	3	3	12	15	27	-12	12

The 2002 Uruguay World Cup Team:

Name of the Coach: Victor Pua

World ranking (January 2002): 24

Approximate betting odds: 80/1

Drawn in Group: A

Country where they will play the group matches: South Korea

Players to watch: Alvaro Recoba, Richard Morales, Dario Silva

Overview of Uruguay:

Hosts of the first World Cup and twice winners, Uruguay are back in the finals after a 12 year absence. The 'celeste' as they are better known decided to take the tough route to qualify having finished 5th in the South American group. Forced to the play offs, they lost 1-0 to Australia in Melbourne, but then won the return leg 3-0 ensuring their tenth appearance in the finals. The majority of the Uruguayan team ply their trade in the lucrative Italian and Spanish leagues, however some do play at home but it is the exception. Like many other South American nations Uruguay changed their coach half way through qualification; Victor Pua replaced the Argentinean Passarella and after much uncertainty is set to take his team to the finals. Players to watch include the sharp shooting Recoba, Dario Silva and the very unpredictable Morales, all of whom will certainly be needed on the 6th June in their tough draw against France.

USA

Capital City: Washington, DC

Location: Stretching across the continent of North America the USA borders Canada to the North and Mexico to the South

Land Mass: 9,160,454 Km Sq

Average monthly income US Dollars: $2,659 Per Month

Currency: 1 US Dollar = 100 Cents

Population: 280 Million

Football in USA:

Year Football Federation was founded: 1913

Number of registered football clubs: 7,000

Number of registered players: 1,411,500

Official website address: www.ussoccer.com

National colours: All white

Previous World Cup Finals Experience:

Previous World Cup finals appearances: 1930, 1934, 1950, 1990, 1994 (Hosts), 1998

Best position in the finals: Semi Finals 1930

Largest victory in the finals: 3-0 V Belgium 1930, V Paraguay 1930

Heaviest defeat in the finals: 1-7 V Italy, 1930

Highest attendance in the finals: 93,869 V Romania, 1994

Lowest attendance in the finals: 800 V Paraguay, 1930

How USA qualified for the World Cup Finals:

How did the qualification process work in USA's continent?

The CONCACAF (Confederation of North Central American and Caribbean Association Football) was probably the most complicated and extensive qualification process. There were three qualification stages - The preliminary phase, the Semi finals and the Final qualification stage. The phases were run on a league basis with Costa Rica, Jamaica, Mexico and USA all getting byes from the first stage having qualified for the World Cup finals before. The final group of six played home and away with the top three in the group qualifying.

Final Position in their group table:

Country	Pl	W	D	L	F	A	GD	Pts
Costa Rica	10	7	2	1	17	7	10	23
Mexico	10	5	2	3	16	9	7	17
USA	*10*	*5*	*2*	*3*	*11*	*8*	*3*	*17*
Honduras	10	4	2	4	17	17	0	14
Jamaica	10	1	2	7	5	18	-13	5
Trinidad	10	1	2	7	5	18	-13	5

The 2002 USA World Cup Team:

Name of the Coach: Bruce Arena

World ranking (January 2002): 20

Approximate betting odds: 150/1

Drawn in Group: D

Country where they will play the group matches: South Korea

Players to watch: Claudio Reyna, Brad Friedel, Joe Max-Moore

Overview of USA:

The US qualify for the finals for the seventh time having navigated the maze of the CONCACAF qualification competition. Soccer in the USA is still growing.The top MLS teams are consistantly getting 20,000 fans a game through their gate, and the export of players is increasing, ultimately bringing much needed experience to the team. None of the games that the USA will play in the round of 32 are easy, they are in a tough group and they know it. Defensively as ever, the USA are strong with either Friedel or Keller in goal. The players to watch are Sunderland's (English Premiership) Claudio Reyna, Joe Max-Moore of Everton (English Premiership) and Earnie Stewart of NAC Breda (Dutch League). Ranked as outsiders, the US will be striving to get to the last 16, but simply appearing in Korea will no doubt help give Soccer a firmer foothold at home.

South Korea

Seoul
Incheon
Suwon
Daejeon
Jeonju
Daegu
Gwangju
Ulsan
Busan
Jeju

South Korea

Useful Tips for the Traveller:

Inoculations: There are no mandatory requirements for inoculations but you should consider vaccinations for hepatitis, typhoid, polio, tetanus and diphtheria.

Currency: The South Korean unit of currency is Won (W). Notes are available in W1,000, W5,000 and W10,000. Coins are available in W1, W5, W10. W50, W100, W500. At the time of writing (Feb 2002) $US 1 was equivalent to W1,300

Travellers Cheques: Travellers cheques are taken readily across South Korea. It is best to take $US as they are the most readily accepted currency.

ATM: Cash advance machines as they are referred to in South Korea are available in most cities. Most Korean bank machines will not take foreign cards and you may have a problem getting your card back. Look out for machines with HanNet or Samsung written above them as they accept all foreign and credit cards.

Tipping: Tipping is not practiced in South Korea.

Temperature: Average Temperatures and Rainfall in the Month of June.

City	Average Temperature	Average Rainfall
Seoul	21.5° Celsius	134 mm
Busan	20.5° Celsius	224 mm
Jeju	21° Celsius	183 mm

Time Zones: South Korea is 9 hours ahead of Greenwich Mean Time and 14 hours ahead of Eastern Standard Time in the USA. There is no daylight saving in South Korea so in the month of June it will be 8 hours ahead of the UK and Ireland.

Visa Requirements: From the UK or Ireland you can visit South Korea Visa free for up to 90 days. From the USA you will be awarded 30 days Visa free before having to extend for up to a further 90 days.

Telephone system: Coin phones are available but you are best using a phonecard as the highest denomination most coin phones take is the W100 coin. Phonecards come in denominations of W2,000, W3,000 W5,000, and W10,000 and are available just about everywhere.

◆ To call The UK, first enter the international access code 001, then dial 44, then the area code minus the first zero and then the number.

◆ To call The Republic of Ireland, first enter the international access code 001, then dial 353, then the area code minus the first zero and then the number.

◆ To call The United States, first enter the international access code 001, then dial 1 then the area code minus the first zero and then the number.

◆ The International dialling code for South Korea is 0082.

Taxation: Value added tax is added to most goods and services at a rate of 10% and is included in the retail price. In hotels, this 10% tax applies to rooms, meals and other services and is added to the bill.

Airport Departure Tax: Known in South Korea as Passenger Service Charge (PSC), all international departures pay W9,000 with children under 2 years of age exempt. Internal flights cost W3,000 but this is automatically added to the price.

Electricity: Most of Korea has now converted to 220V 60 cycles per second (distinguishable by two round pins) but you may find some power outlets at 110V 60 cycles per second (distinguishable by two flat pins). All outlets are of US type.

Emergency Telephone Numbers:

Dial 112 for Police

Dial 119 for Fire or Ambulance

Dial 080 211 0114 for the English operator.

If you are using a public telephone push the red button before you enter the emergency number and it will connect for free.

Some Useful Phrases:

Thank You.	Gamsa Hamnida
Please help me?	Dowa-juseyo
Where is (x) ?	(x)i eodi itseumnikka
How much is it ?	Geougeoseun eolma-imnikka
Do you have a Vacancy?	Bin bang itseumnikka
Airport.	Gong hang
Train station.	Gichayeok
Subway.	Jihacheol
Hotel.	Hotel

I am visiting South Korea to watch the World Cup.

Na Neun world cup gu kyung ha reo go han gook e ya eum ni da.

Busan Stadium

Stadium Address: 1300 Geoje Dong, Yeonje Gu, Busan Metropolitan City

Telephone number: 0082 51 973 100 Gimhae Tourist Information Centre

Capacity: 62,685

Website: www.metro.pusan.kr

General comments on the stadium:

Built to symbolise the globe, the Busan Stadium took 10 years to build and will play host to the World Cup and the Asian Games of 2002. With all seating covered, this multi purpose stadium is constructed over 6 levels; 4 above ground and 2 below.

Travelling there:

Nearest Airport: Gimhae International (16Km from the stadium)

Nearest Train Station: Busan Station (13Km from the stadium)

Nearest Subway Station: Dongnae Subway Station

Directions: Access to the stadium is best reached by a 20 minute walk from the Dongnae subway station which is on Subway Line 1 (there are only 2 lines). Alternatively you can reach Busan via one of the numerous bus routes from the Express Bus terminal.

Daegu Stadium

Stadium Address:
504 Naehwan Dong,
Suseong Gu, Daegu
Metropolitan City

Telephone Number:
0082 53 627 8900 Daegu
Tourist Information Centre

Capacity: 70,140

Website: www.metro.taegu.kr

General comments on the stadium:

Hosts to the 2001 Confederations cup and next
years 2003 Universaid games, Daegu is a multi
purpose 75% covered stadium.

Travelling there:

Nearest Airport: Daegu International Airport
(11Km)

Nearest Train Station: East Deagu (5Km)/
Dongdaegu Stations

Nearest Subway Station: Singi - Subway Line one

Directions: Daegu boasts an extensive transportation
network. Plane, train, subway or express bus will get
you to Daegu. The easiest way to get to the stadium
is to take the Subway line 1 to Singi station and follow
the directions of the numerous guides.

Daejeon Stadium

Stadium Address:
270 Noeun Dong,
Yuseong-gu, Daejeon

Telephone Number:
0082 42226 7788. Daejeon
Transport Information

Capacity: 41,651

Website: www.metro.taejon.kr

General comments on the stadium:

Taking just under 3 years to complete, Daejeon has been constructed exclusively for football. 58% covered with a retractable roof, the stadium will be used by the local football team Daejeon Citizen on completion of the World Cup.

Travelling there:

Nearest Airport: Cheongju International Airport

Nearest Train Station: Daejeon (9Km) or Seo Daejeon (11Km)

Nearest Subway Station: Not Applicable

Directions: Daejeon is located 150Km South of Seoul. If driving, take the Kyungbu / Honam highway; there are 3,200 parking spaces at the ground. From Daejeon Station take either the 104 or 140 bus to Daejeon World Cup stadium. From Seo Daejeon train station take bus number 101 to the same location.

Gwangju Stadium

Stadium Address:
423-2, Pungam-dong,
Seo-gu, Gwangju

Telephone Number: 0082
51973 100 Gwangju
Tourist information centre

Capacity: 42,880

Website: www.metro.kwangju.kr

General comments on the stadium:

60% covered and a stadium intended purely for
football, Gwangju's literature deems it the 'stadium
of light'. Two eliptical wings provide the roofing, set
over 5 stories and with a golf course, swimming
pool, auxiliary stadium and horse riding area,
Gwangju was constructed with no expense spared!

Travelling there:

Nearest Airport: Gwangju Airport

Nearest Train Station: Gwangju Station

Nearest Subway Station: Not Available

Directions: From Gwangju Airport take the 106
bus. From Gwangju Train station and the bus
terminal take the number 36 bus. Parking is
available at the stadium with 4,300 spaces.

Incheon Stadium

Stadium Address: San 8 Munhak-dong, Nam-gu, Incheon

Telephone Number: 0082 32 884 4590 Tourist information centre

Capacity: 52,179

Website: www.metro.inchon.kr

General comments on the stadium:

The stadium took just over 7 years to build and has been constructed as a sports complex with athletics facilities. There are a multitude of fitness suites, training centres and also a large number of dining facilities along with accommodation! The roofing (which covers 100% of the stadium) is designed to resemble ships sails and masts as Incheon city is historically known as the gateway to the sea.

Travelling there:

Nearest Airport: Incheon International Airport

Nearest Train Station: Incheon Station

Nearest Subway Station: Munhak Stadium station

Directions: The easiest way to reach the stadium is by taking the subway to Munhak stadium station and then walking for 15 minutes (if you are coming from Seoul, take Subway Line 1 to Bupyeong Station and transfer to the Incheon subway system and alight at Munhak station). From Incheon or Gimpo airport, limousine buses run every 15 minutes direct to the stadium. To take the bus from downtown Incheon use numbers 4,6,13 or 27 which go via the stadium.

Jeonju Stadium

Stadium Address: 763-1 Banwol-dong, Deokjin-gu, Jeonju-si, Jeollabuk-do

Telephone Number: 0082 63580 4434 Tourist information centre

Capacity: 42,371

Website: www.chonju.chonbuk.kr

General comments on the stadium:

Jeonju is a large sports complex which covers an enormous 620,000 Meters Sq. Jeonju has been built full of local symbolism; the roof which covers 85% of the seating is shaped to signify wings and a Korean fan, the cables that hold up the roof signify a local 12 stringed musical instrument and the poles signify a prayer pole wishing for a good harvest.

Travelling there:

Nearest Airport: Gunsan Airport

Nearest Train Station: Jeonju Station

Nearest Subway Station: Not Available

Directions: From Gunsan Airport, take the express bus to Jeonju and then change at the city bus terminal on to the 225, 228, 336, 337 or 556 for the stadium. From Jeonju train station take the 70-5 and the 79-1 to the bus interchange and then take the 225, 228, 336, 337 or 556 for the stadium. From the express bus terminal, take the 225 or 336 to the stadium.

Jeju Stadium

Stadium Address: 914 Beophwan-dong, Seogwipo-si, Jejudo Island

Telephone Number: 0082 64742 8866 Jejudo Tourist information

Capacity: 42,256

Website: www.sogwipo.cheju.kr

General comments on the stadium:

The Jeju Stadium is located in Seogwipo City which is located on the Jejudo Island on the Southern tip of the Korean Peninsula. The stadium has a large crescent shaped roof which covers 50% of the seating and is built to symbolise a volcano crater. Completed in December 2001, the stadium will be used for a variety of commercial purposes after the World Cup including the possible construction of an IMAX cinema.

Travelling there:

Nearest Airport: Jeju Airport

Nearest Train Station: Not Available

Nearest Subway Station: Not Available

Directions: From the Airport, take one of the many available Limousine buses to the stadium (Approx 60 Minutes). From Seogwipo Intercity Bus Terminal take buses 6,11,110,120,130, 200 or 400 to the stadium. There is no subway or train station near the stadium and parking is very limited (700 places).

Seoul Stadium

Stadium Address: 515 Seongsan-dong, Mapo-gu, Seoul

Telephone Number: 0082 22236 9135 General Information

Capacity: 63,930

Website: www.metro.seoul.kr

General comments on the stadium:

Seoul is a newly constructed state of the art stadium with amazing lighting and interior layout. The roof is shaped like a large rectangular shield styled like a Korean kite. The whole stadium is supposed to symbolise unity and the future hope of unification for the Korean people.

Travelling there:

Nearest Airport: Gimpo or Incheon Airports

Nearest Train Station: Seoul Station

Nearest Subway Station: World Cup Stadium Station

Directions: The subway is by far the most efficient way of getting to the stadium. Using the newly constructed Line number 6, take it as far as World Cup station and then walk for 5 minutes to the stadium. The stadium is 42Km from Incheon airport and 13Km from Gimpo airport. Taxis and airport Limousines are plentiful but check the price before you depart.

Suwon Stadium

Stadium Address: 228 Uman-dong, Paldal-gu, Suwon-si, Gyeonggi-do

Telephone Number: 0082 31228 2785 Sunwon tourist information centre

Capacity: 43,188

Website: www.suwon.kyonggi.kr

General comments on the stadium:

Suwon is a stadium constructed solely for football but also boasts a sports complex on it's site. The sports complex houses an auxiliary stadium, 2 practice fields, cultural centres, swimming pools and tennis courts. After the World Cup it will be used by the professional Korean football team, the Samsung Blue Wings. The most unusual feature of the stadium is the roof which is shaped as a wing meant to symbolize the future and the image of the stadium floating into the sky.

Travelling there:

Nearest Airport: Gimpo Airport (60Km), Incheon International Airport (80Km)

Nearest Train Station: Suwon Station

Nearest Subway Station: Not Available

Directions: From Suwon train station take bus numbers 2 or 13-2 to the stadium which will take 20-30 minutes. Airport limousine buses from both airports take approximately 90 minutes. If driving, use the East Suwon or Shingal Interchanges (expressways), there are 2,748 parking places at the stadium.

Ulsan Stadium

Stadium Address: San 5,
Ok-dong, Nam-gu, Ulsan

Telephone Number:
0082 52 277 0101 Tourist
information centre

Capacity: 42,086

Website: www.metro.ulsam.kr

General comments on the stadium:

Ulsan is the industrial capital of South Korea.
The stadium has been built to symbolize this link,
emphasizing the mechanical and industrial aspects
of the city along with it's emphasis upon the
environmentally friendly. Another sports complex
covering a huge 900,000 Meters Sq, Ulsan also
houses racquetball courts, bowling alleys, a table
tennis court and a fitness centre. Ulsan is known
as the Korean football Mecca and visitors will
undoubtedly be made to feel very welcome.

Travelling there:

Nearest Airport: Ulsan Airport

Nearest Train Station: Ulsan Station

Nearest Subway Station: Not Available

Directions: From Ulsan Airport, take bus numbers
20, 24, 120 or 124 to the stadium, which should take
approximately 45 minutes. From the train station,
buses 102, 112, 126 and 1-2 will get you to the stadium
in 25 minutes. From the bus terminal take the 1-2, 29,
38, 102, 127 or 513 which will also take 25 minutes.
If you wish to drive, there are 4,000 parking places.

Japan

Useful Tips for the Traveller:

Inoculations: No compulsory immunisations or health certificates are required to enter the country. Malaria is not endemic in Japan.

Currency: The Japanese currency is the Yen (¥). Notes are available in ¥1000, ¥2000, ¥5000, ¥10,000. Coins are available in ¥1, ¥5, ¥10, ¥50, ¥100 and ¥500. At the time of writing (Feb 2002) $US 1 was equivalent to ¥131

Travellers Cheques: Travellers Cheques are accepted across the country and unusually attract a better rate of exchange than cash.

ATM: ATM machines are becoming more common. It is best to look for an 'International ATM' as this will also have an English language facility.

Tipping: Tipping is not practiced in Japan.

Temperature: Average Temperatures and Rainfall in the Month of June.

City	Average Temperature	AverageRainfall
Naha	27° Celsius	300 mm
Fukuoka	24° Celsius	250 mm
Osaka	25° Celsius	210 mm
Tokyo	25° Celsius	180 mm
Sendai	19° Celsius	140 mm
Sapporo	19° Celsius	80 mm

Time Zones: Japan is 9 hours ahead of Greenwich Mean Time and 14 hours ahead of Eastern Standard Time in the USA. There is no daylight saving in Japan so in the month of June it will be 8 hours ahead of the UK and Ireland.

Visa Requirements: Citizens of the UK and Ireland do not require a visa and will be able to stay for up to 90 days without one. If an extension is then required you must visit one of the many immigration bureaux's and a further 90 days will be given. If you are a US citizen, no visa is required for the first 90 days of your stay, however if you wish to apply for a further 90 days you will need to exit the country and re-enter.

Telephone system: You are always very close to a phone in Japan and you can use either coins or phone cards. Check with the phone to ensure it has the capability to work internationally and that the maximum coin denomination is above ¥100. Otherwise use phonecards, which can be purchased, from most shops.

◆ To call The UK, dial 0044, then the area code minus the first zero and then the number.

◆ To call The Republic of Ireland, dial 00353, then the area code minus the first zero and then the number.

◆ To call The United States, dial 01 then the area code minus the first zero and then the number.

◆ The International dialling code for Japan is 0081

Taxation: A consumption tax of 5% is added to just about all goods and services. It is often added within the price and other times added on top so it is always best to ask before a bill is paid. Some of the very luxurious hotels add a 10% service charge but this is unusual.

Airport Departure Tax: A departure tax of ¥2650 (¥1330 for children) is payable on departure from Kansai International airport. If leaving from Narita Airport you will have to pay ¥2040 (¥1020 for children)

Electricity: The electrical current is 100v, 50Hz in East Japan (including Tokyo). 100v, 60Hz in Western Japan. If travelling from North America, you will need a transformer.

Emergency Telephone Numbers:

Dial 110 for the Police

Dial 119 For an Ambulance or the Fire Brigade

The Tokyo Metropolitan Police operate an English Language hotline on 03 3501 0110 if you are unsuccessful calling the above.

Some Useful Phrases:

Thank You	Domo arigato
Can you please help me?	Tetusudatte kuremansen ka
Where is (x) ?	(x) wa doko desu ka

I don't speak Japanese.	Nihongo wa Yomimasen
How much is it ?	Kore wa ikura desu ka
Do you have any Vacancies?	Aita heya wa arimasu ka
Airport.	Kuko
Train.	Densha
Subway.	Chikatetsu
Hotel.	Hoteru

I am visiting Japan for the World Cup.
Watashiwa world cup no tame Nippon e ikimasu

I am a fan of (x) football team.
Watishiwa (x) no fan desu

Ibaraki Stadium

Stadium Address:
26-2 Ushiroyama, Jinkoji,
Kashima City, Ibaraki

Telephone Number:
(0081) 0298 21 4168

Capacity: 42,000

Website: www.pref.iberaki.jp

General comments on the stadium:

Ibaraki stadium received a face lift during
2000/2001 and an extra 26,000 seats were added
by including another tier of seating. Home to the
Kashima Antlers (J League Champions 2000), a
large viewing screen and improved drainage have
also been added to the stadium.

Travelling there:

Nearest Airport: Narita International Airport

Nearest Train Station: Kashima Soccer
Stadium Station

Nearest Subway Station: Not Available

Directions: By train, alight at Kashima Soccer
Stadium station from the JR Kashima line or the
Kashima Rinkai line. You will see the stadium in
front of you and it is no more than a five minute
walk. With 12,000 parking spaces, you can drive,
but check routes as there are a number of
alternatives from Tokyo.

Kobe Wing Stadium

Stadium Address: 1 Misaki-cho, Hyogu-ku, Kobe City

Telephone Number: (0081) 078 322 0220

Capacity: 42,000

Website: www.city.kobe.jp

General comments on the stadium:

Kobe stadium has been constructed specifically for the World Cup. The use of the word wing in it's title is used to conjure up the image of wings rising from the reconstruction of the terrible Kobe Earthquake of 1995. With a retractable roof and in stadium heating, Kobe has been designed for comfort

Travelling there:

Nearest Airport: Kansai International Airport or Osaka Airport

Nearest Train Station: Shin Kobe Station and then link by Subway (2 Mins) to Sannomiya Station (City Centre).

Nearest Subway Station: Misaki-keon Stadium on the Kobe City Subway Kaigan Line

Directions: Having arrived by plane or train, it is best to head for the very efficient subway system. Misaki-keon station is easy to find on the subway Kaigan Line. If travelling by car there is limited parking at the stadium (1,470 places).

Miyagi Stadium

Stadium Address: 40-1 Aza Tate, Sugaya, Rifu-cho, Miyagi

Telephone Number: (0081) 022 211 2822

Capacity: 49,291

Website: www.pref.miyagi.jp

General comments on the stadium:

Miyagi is a multi purpose stadium which can be used for all major sporting events including athletics. The stadium was designed with a sweeping half moon shaped grandstand to replicate the battle helmet of the 'Date Clan' who ruled Japan during the feudal period. A state of the art stadium, Miyagi especially prides it's self on it's excellent facilities for the handicapped and hard of hearing.

Travelling there:

Nearest Airport: Sendai Airport

Nearest Train Station: JR Iwakiri Station

Nearest Subway Station: Not Available

Directions: Located 10Km outside of Sendai City, take the Bullet (JR) train from Sendai City on the Tohoku Honsen Line to JR Iwakiri Station. You will then be able to get a shuttle bus to the stadium which is a 10 Minute drive away. If driving, take the Tohoku Expressway to downtown Sendai and then follow directions to the stadium (30 Mins).

Niigata Big Swan Stadium

Stadium Address: 68, Seigoro, Niigata City, Niigata

Telephone Number: (0081) 025 285 5511

Capacity: 42,300

Website: www.pref.niigata.jp

General comments on the stadium:

The big swan stadium was inspired by the nearby Toyanogata Lagoon, which is used by bird watchers to watch the numerous swans that live on it. The curves of the stadium are supposed to symbalise the 'symmetry' of a swan. The 42,300 seater stadium is 90% covered by a see-through roof which allows natural light into the stadium complex.

Travelling there:

Nearest Airport: Niigata Airport

Nearest Train Station: JR (Bullet Train) Niigata station

Nearest Subway Station: Not available

Directions: Located 4Km out of Niigata City Centre, the stadium is best reached by shuttle bus. Buses are available from the airport and also from JR Niigata station. There are 4,000 parking spaces by the stadium which is best reached by the Kanetsu Expressway.

Oita Stadium Big Eye

Stadium Address: Yokoo, Matsuoka, Oita City

Telephone Number: (0081) 097 536 1111

Capacity: 43,000

Website: www2.pref.oita.jp

General comments on the stadium:

The Big Eye stadium has been designed in the shape of a globe (when the retractable roof is closed) to promote 'environmental protection'. Oita has 9,000 moveable seats to enable it to transform into an athletics stadium or Rugby pitch, it also boasts sky cameras which move to give a variety of differing pictures which are transmitted on a large internal screen.

Travelling there:

Nearest Airport: Oita Airport

Nearest Train Station: Oita Stadium

Nearest Subway Station: Not available

Directions: The Southern most of Japan's ten stadiums, Oita has excellent transport links. From the Airport take the hovercraft (20 mins) or bus (60 mins) to the city centre. From the city centre by car or taxi will take 30 mins. By train, take the direct link to Oita Stadium (if coming from Tokyo change first at Kokura station).

Osaka Stadium

Stadium Address: 1-1 Nagai Koen, Higashisumiyoshi-ku, Osaka City

Telephone Number: (0081) 06 6305 3311

Capacity: 50,000

Website: www.osakacity.or.jp

General comments on the stadium:

Renovated in 1996, the Osaka stadium is a multi purpose centre for a variety of sporting events. With a 9 lane, 400 metre athletics track and a football pitch that doubles up as an athletics field, Osaka is very large and very impressive. The stadium has been designed with no beams to ensure that the whole of the pitch can be viewed from every seat.

Travelling there:

Nearest Airport: Kansai International Airport

Nearest Train Station: Osaka Station

Nearest Subway Station: Nagai Station (on the Midosuji line)

Directions: The stadium is approximately 10Km from the city centre and the best way to reach it is by using the subway. On the subway alight at Nagai station on the Midosuji Line and the stadium is no more than 10 minutes walk. If you wish to drive (not recommended) there are 2,500 parking spaces at the ground.

Saitama Stadium

Stadium Address:
Oazamnakanoda-Chinai,
Urawa-shi, Saitama-Ken

Telephone Number:
(0081) 048 830 3955

Capacity: 63,700

Website: www.pref.saitama.jp

General comments on the stadium:

Saitama is Asia's largest football only stadium.
Utilising technology, the stadium uses solar
powered generators and has a system of collecting
rainwater from the roof to water the pitch. Located
only 50 minutes from Tokyo and situated in the
soccer mad area of Urawa, demand for tickets at
Saitama will be very high.

Travelling there:

Nearest Airport: Narita Airport

Nearest Train Station: JR Urawa Misono Station

Nearest Subway Station: Not Available

Directions: Taking the Bullet train to JR Urawa
Misono station is probably the easiest way of getting
to Saitama Stadium. The stadium is a 15 minute
walk and is well signposted. With 2,500 Parking
spaces, the stadium can also be reached by road
using the Kan'etsu and Tohoku expressways.

Sapporo Dome Stadium

Stadium Address: 1-3 Hitsujigaoka, Toyohira-ku, Sapporo City

Telephone Number: (0081) 011 211 3341

Capacity: 42,000

Website: www.global.city.sapporo.jp

General comments on the stadium:

Sapporo Dome is truly an amazing stadium. Because of the heavy snow in the winter, Sapporo dome has been designed complete with roof and changeable pitch. The natural grass pitch can be pushed outside on an air cushion and an artificial one put in it's place. It is fully airconditioned in the summer and during the winter seats are heated.

Travelling there:

Nearest Airport: Sapporo (New Chitose) Airport

Nearest Train Station: Sapporo Station

Nearest Subway Station: Fukuzumi Station

Directions: Using the Subway is the easiest method. Take the Toho Subway line to Fukuzumi station and then walk 10 minutes to the stadium. Alternatively take a taxi from Sapporo station which will take 30 Minutes. There are also 1,700 parking spaces by the stadium.

Shizuoka Stadium Ecopa

Stadium Address:
Ogasayama Sports Park,
Aino, Fukori City

Telephone Number:
(0081) 054 255 1388

Capacity: 50,600

Website: www.shizuokanet.ne.jp/worldcup/english

General comments on the stadium:

A multi purpose stadium with athletics track and field. Shizuoka stadium was constructed to incorporate the image of the nearby Ogasayama Mountains. Surrounded by amazing natural beauty Mount Fuji (the highest mountain in Japan) is a mere 10 minute drive away.

Travelling there:

Nearest Airport: Nagoya or Tokyo Airport

Nearest Train Station: JR Tokaido

Nearest Subway Station: Not Available

Directions: Shizuoka Stadium is located 50Km outside of the city centre. If travelling by car, take the Tomei Expressway and park in one of the stadiums 3,695 parking places. Travelling by train take the JR (Bullet Train) from the city centre and alight at the Tokaido Line station. The stadium is then a 10 minute walk.

Yokohama Stadium

Stadium Address: 3302-5 Kozukoe, Kohoku-ku, Yokahama City

Telephone Number: (0081) 045 441 7300

Capacity: 72,370

Website: www.city.yokohama.jp/front/welcomeE.html

General comments on the stadium:

World Cup Final venue and largest stadium in Japan, Yokohama also has an athletics pitch and field and has hosted American Football and Rugby games. Viewing is enhanced by 2 enormous display screens relaying pictures broadcast from a high speed camera that traverses the stadium (travels 100 meters in 7 seconds). Seven stories in height and with a 171,000 Meter Sq area, Yokohama has the largest capacity of all the World Cup Stadiums.

Travelling there:

Nearest Airport: Haneda or Narita Airports

Nearest Train Station: Kozukue Station on the JR Yokohama line

Nearest Subway Station: Shin - Yokohama Station

Directions: Use either the JR Train (bullet) on the Yokohama line, alighting at Kozukue station and walking for 10 minutes to the station. Or take the metropolitan subway getting off at Shin - Yokohama station and walking for 15 minutes to the stadium. There are 3,500 parking spaces but driving is not recommended.

FANFARE
2002
WORLD CUP
GUIDE

The Competition

Group A

Played in: South Korea

Competing Teams:
Denmark Uruguay
Senegal France

DATE	COUNTRY	SCORE		COUNTRY	VENUE
Friday 31 May	Senegal	1	0	France	Seoul (P. 177)
Saturday 1 June	Denmark	2	1	Uruguay	Ulsan (P.179)
Thursday 6 June	Denmark	1	1	Senegal	Daegu (P. 171)
Thursday 6 June	France	0	0	Uruguay	Busan (P. 170)
Tuesday 11 June	Uruguay	3	3	Senegal	Suwon (P. 178)
Tuesday 11 June	France	0	2	Denmark	Incheon (P. 174)

Group A Table:

Three points are awarded for a team win, 1 point is awarded to each team for a draw/tie and 0 points are awarded for a loss. Goal difference is calculated by setting the Goals for (+) from the Goals against (-). For example if Japan have 10 goals for and 4 against they will have a goal difference of +6, if Spain have 3 goals for and 7 goals against they will have a goal difference of -4. If points are drawn/tied after all games have been played then the highest positive (+) goal difference wins.

Team	Won	Drawn/ tie	Lost	Goals For (+)	Goals Against (-)	+/-	Points	Result
DENMARK	2	1	0	5	2		7	AW
SENEGAL	1	2	0	5	4		5	AR
URUGUAY	0	2	1	4	5		2	
FRANCE	0	1	2	0	3		1	

Now enter AW team name on page 204 and AR team name on page 204

Group B
Played in: South Korea

Competing Teams:
Paraguay   Spain
S. Africa   Slovenia

DATE	COUNTRY	SCORE		COUNTRY	VENUE	
Sun 2 June	S. Africa	2	2	Paraguay	Busan	(P. 170)
Sun 2 June	Slovenia	1	3	Spain	Gwangju	(P. 173)
Fri 7 June	Spain	3	1	Paraguay	Jeonju	(P. 175)
Sat 8 June	S. Africa	1	0	Slovenia	Daegu	(P. 171)
Wed 12 June	Paraguay	3	1	Slovenia	Jeju	(P. 176)
Wed 12 June	Spain	3	2	S. Africa	Daejeon	(P. 172)

Group B Table:
Three points are awarded for a team win, 1 point is awarded to each team for a draw/tie and 0 points are awarded for a loss. Goal difference is calculated by setting the Goals for (+) from the Goals against (-). For example if Japan have 10 goals for and 4 against they will have a goal difference of +6, if Spain have 3 goals for and 7 goals against they will have a goal difference of -4. If points are drawn/tied after all games have been played then the highest positive (+) goal difference wins.

Team	Won	Drawn/tie	Lost	Goals For (+)	Goals Against (-)	+/-	Points	Result
SPAIN	3	0	0	9	4		9	BW
PARAGUAY	1	1	1	6	6		4	BR
SOUTH AFRICA	1	1	1	5	5		4	
SLOVENIA	0	0	3	2	7		0	

Now enter BW team name on page 204 and BR team name on page 204

197

Group C
Played in: South Korea

Competing Teams:	
Brazil	C. Rica
Turkey	China

DATE	COUNTRY	SCORE		COUNTRY	VENUE	
Mon 3 June	**Turkey**	1	2	**Brazil**	Ulsan	(P. 179)
Tue 4 June	**China**	0	2	**C. Rica**	Gwangju	(P. 173)
Sat 8 June	**Brazil**	4	0	**China**	Jeju	(P.176)
Sun 9 June	**Turkey**	1	1	**C. Rica**	Incheon	(P. 174)
Thur 13 June	**Brazil**	5	2	**C. Rica**	Suwon	(P. 178)
Thur 13 June	**Turkey**	3	0	**China**	Seoul	(P. 177)

Group C Table:
Three points are awarded for a team win, 1 point is awarded to each team for a draw/tie and 0 points are awarded for a loss. Goal difference is calculated by setting the Goals for (+) from the Goals against (-). For example if Japan have 10 goals for and 4 against they will have a goal difference of +6, if Spain have 3 goals for and 7 goals against they will have a goal difference of -4. If points are drawn/tied after all games have been played then the highest positive (+) goal difference wins.

Team	Won	Drawn/ tie	Lost	Goals For (+)	Goals Against (-)	+/-	Points	Result
BRAZIL	3	0	0	11	3		9	CW
TURKEY	1	1	1	5	3		4	CR
COSTA RICA	1	1	1	5	6		4	
CHINA	0	0	3	0	9		0	

Now enter CW team name on page 205 and CR team name on page 205

Group D

Played in: South Korea

	Competing Teams:	
S. Korea	**USA**	
Poland	**Portugal**	

DATE	COUNTRY	SCORE		COUNTRY	VENUE	
Tue 4 June	S. Korea	2	0	Poland	Busan	(P. 170)
Wed 5 June	Portugal	2	3	USA	Suwon	(P. 178)
Mon 10 June	Portugal	4	0	Poland	Jeonju	(P. 175)
Mon 10 June	S. Korea	1	1	USA	Daegu	(P. 171)
Fri 14 June	Poland	3	1	USA	Daejeon	(P. 172)
Fri 14 June	Portugal	0	1	S. Korea	Incheon	(P. 174)

Group D Table:

Three points are awarded for a team win, 1 point is awarded to each team for a draw/tie and 0 points are awarded for a loss. Goal difference is calculated by setting the Goals for (+) from the Goals against (-). For example if Japan have 10 goals for and 4 against they will have a goal difference of +6, if Spain have 3 goals for and 7 goals against they will have a goal difference of -4. If points are drawn/tied after all games have been played then the highest positive (+) goal difference wins.

Team	Won	Drawn/tie	Lost	Goals For (+)	Goals Against (-)	+/-	Points	Result
SOUTH KOREA	2	1	0	4	1		7	DW
UNITED STATES	1	1	1	5	6		4	DR
PORTUGAL	1	0	2	6	4		3	
POLAND	1	0	2	3	7		-3	

Now enter DW team name on page 205 and DR team name on page 205

199

Group E
Played in: Japan

	Competing Teams:
	Ireland Germany
	Cameroon S. Arabia

DATE	COUNTRY	SCORE		COUNTRY	VENUE	
Sat 1 June	Cameroon	1	1	Ireland	Niigata	(P. 188)
Sat 1 June	S. Arabia	0	8	Germany	Sapporo	(P. 192)
Wed 5 June	Germany	1	1	Ireland	Ibaraki	(P. 185)
Thur 6 June	Cameroon	1	0	S. Arabia	Saitama	(P. 191)
Tue 11 June	Ireland	3	0	S. Arabia	Yokohama	(P. 194)
Tue 11 June	Cameroon	0	2	Germany	Shizuoka	(P. 193)

Group E Table:
Three points are awarded for a team win, 1 point is awarded to each team for a draw/tie and 0 points are awarded for a loss. Goal difference is calculated by setting the Goals for (+) from the Goals against (-). For example if Japan have 10 goals for and 4 against they will have a goal difference of +6, if Spain have 3 goals for and 7 goals against they will have a goal difference of -4. If points are drawn/tied after all games have been played then the highest positive (+) goal difference wins.

Team	Won	Drawn/tie	Lost	Goals For (+)	Goals Against (-)	+/-	Points	Result
GERMANY	2	1	0	11	1		7	EW
REP OF IRELAND	1	2	0	5	2		5	ER
CAMEROON	1	1	1	2	3		4	
SAUDI ARABIA	0	0	3	0	12		0	

Now enter EW team name on page 204 and ER team name on page 204

Group F
Played in: Japan

Competing Teams:	
England	Argentina
Sweden	Nigeria

DATE	COUNTRY	SCORE	COUNTRY	VENUE	
Sun 2 June	**Nigeria**	0 1	**Argentina**	Ibaraki	(P. 185)
Sun 2 June	**England**	1 1	**Sweden**	Saitama	(P. 191)
Fri 7 June	**Sweden**	2 1	**Nigeria**	Kobe	(P. 186)
Fri 7 June	**Argentina**	0 1	**England**	Sapporo	(P. 192)
Wed 12 June	**Nigeria**	0 0	**England**	Osaka	(P. 190)
Wed 12 June	**Sweden**	1 1	**Argentina**	Miyagi	(P. 187)

Group F Table:
Three points are awarded for a team win, 1 point is awarded to each team for a draw/tie and 0 points are awarded for a loss. Goal difference is calculated by setting the Goals for (+) from the Goals against (-). For example if Japan have 10 goals for and 4 against they will have a goal difference of +6, if Spain have 3 goals for and 7 goals against they will have a goal difference of -4. If points are drawn/tied after all games have been played then the highest positive (+) goal difference wins.

Team	Won	Drawn/tie	Lost	Goals For (+)	Goals Against (-)	+/-	Points	Result
SWEDEN	1	2	0	4	3		5	FW
ENGLAND	1	2	0	2	1		5	FR
ARGENTINA	1	1	1	2	2		4	
NIGERIA	0	1	2	1	3		1	

Now enter FW team name on page 204 and FR team name on page 204

201

Group G
Played in: Japan

	Competing Teams:
Croatia	Ecuador
Italy	Mexico

DATE	COUNTRY	SCORE		COUNTRY	VENUE
Mon 3 June	Mexico	1	0	Croatia	Niigata *(P.188)*
Mon 3 June	Ecuador	0	2	Italy	Sapporo *(P.192)*
Sat 8 June	Italy	1	2	Croatia	Ibaraki *(P.185)*
Sun 9 June	Mexico	2	1	Ecuador	Miyagi *(P.187)*
Thur 13 June	Croatia	0	1	Ecuador	Yokohama *(P.194)*
Thur 13 June	Mexico	1	1	Italy	Oita *(P.189)*

Group G Table:
Three points are awarded for a team win, 1 point is awarded to each team for a draw/tie and 0 points are awarded for a loss. Goal difference is calculated by setting the Goals for (+) from the Goals against (-). For example if Japan have 10 goals for and 4 against they will have a goal difference of +6, if Spain have 3 goals for and 7 goals against they will have a goal difference of -4. If points are drawn/tied after all games have been played then the highest positive (+) goal difference wins.

Team	Won	Drawn/tie	Lost	Goals For (+)	Goals Against (-)	+/-	Points	Result
MEXICO	2	1	0	4	2		7	GW
ITALY	1	1	1	4	3		4	GR
CROATIA	1	0	2	2	3		3	
EQUADOR	1	0	2	2	4		3	

Now enter GW team name on page 205 and GR team name on page 205

Group H

Played in: Japan

Competing Teams:	
Belgium	Russia
Japan	Tunisia

DATE	COUNTRY	SCORE		COUNTRY	VENUE	
Tue 4 June	Japan	2	2	Belgium	Saitama	(P.191)
Wed 5 June	Russia	2	0	Tunisia	Kobe	(P.186)
Sun 9 June	Japan	1	0	Russia	Yokohama	(P.194)
Mon 10 June	Tunisia	1	1	Belgium	Oita	(P.189)
Fri 14 June	Belgium	3	2	Russia	Shizuoka	(P.193)
Fri 14 June	Japan	2	0	Tunisia	Osaka	(P.190)

Group H Table:

Three points are awarded for a team win, 1 point is awarded to each team for a draw/tie and 0 points are awarded for a loss. Goal difference is calculated by setting the Goals for (+) from the Goals against (-). For example if Japan have 10 goals for and 4 against they will have a goal difference of +6, if Spain have 3 goals for and 7 goals against they will have a goal difference of -4. If points are drawn/tied after all games have been played then the highest positive (+) goal difference wins.

Team	Won	Drawn/ tie	Lost	Goals For (+)	Goals Against (-)	+/-	Points	Result
JAPAN	2	1	0	5	2		7	HW
BELGIUM	1	2	0	6	5		5	HR
RUSSIA	1	0	2	4	4		4	
TUNISIA	0	1	2	1	5		1	

Now enter HW team name on page 205 and HR team name on page 205

Match Number 1:

EW GERMANY	1	0	BR PARAGUAY

Saturday 15th June
Played at Jeju (See Page 176)
Now enter the winner of the match in line Q3 on page 206

Match Number 2: DENMARK   ENGLAND

AW ~~MEXICO~~	0	3	FR USA

Saturday 15th June
Played at Niigata (See Page 188)
Now enter the winner of the match in line Q1 on page 206

Match Number 3:

FW SWEDEN	0	2	AR SENEGAL

Sunday 16th June
Played at Oita (See Page 189)
Now enter the winner of the match in line Q7 on page 206

Match Number 4:

BW SPAIN	1	1	ER IRELAND

Sunday 16th June
Played at Suwon (See Page 178)
Now enter the winner of the match in line Q5 on page 206

↳ WON ON PENALTIES

204

Match Number 5:

GW MEXICO	0	2	DR USA

Monday 17th June
Played at Jeonju (See Page 175)
Now enter the winner of the match in line Q4 on page 206

Match Number 6:

CW BRAZIL	2	0	HR BELGUIM

Monday 17th June
Played at Kobe (See Page 186)
Now enter the winner of the match in line Q2 on page 206

Match Number 7:

HW JAPAN	0	1	CR TURKEY

Tuesday 18th June
Played at Miyagi (See Page 187)
Now enter the winner of the match in line Q8 on page 206

Match Number 8:

DW STH KOREA	2	1	GR ITALY

Tuesday 18th June
Played at Daejeon (See Page 172)
Now enter the winner of the match in line Q6 on page 206

Match A:

Q1 ENGLAND	0	1	Q2 BRAZIL

Friday 21st June
Played at Shizuoka (See Page 193)
Now enter the winner of the match in line S3 on page 207

Match B:

Q3 GERMANY	1	0	Q4 USA

Friday 21st June
Played at Ulsan (See Page 179)
Now enter the winner of the match in line S1 on page 207

Match C:

Q5 SPAIN	0	0	Q6 STH KOREA

Saturday 22nd June
Played at Gwangju (See Page 173)
Now enter the winner of the match in line S2 on page 207

STH KOREA WON ON PENALTIES 5-3

Match D:

Q7 SENEGAL	0	1	Q8 TURKEY

Saturday 22nd June
Played at Osaka (See Page 190)
Now enter the winner of the match in line S4 on page 207

Match 1:

S1	GERMANY			S2	5TH KOREA

Tuesday 25th June
Played at Seoul (See Page 177)
Now enter the winner of the match in line F1 on page 208
Enter the name of the losing team below on line T1

Match 2:

S3	BRAZIL			S4	TURKEY

Wednesday 26th June
Played at Saitama (See Page 191)
Now enter the winner of the match in line F2 on page 208
Enter the name of the losing team below on line T2

Third Place Playoff:

T1	TURKEY	3	2	T2	5TH KOREA

Saturday 29th June
Played at Daegu (See Page 171)

3rd Place Winner:

TURKEY

| F1 BRAZIL | 2 | 0 | F2 GERMANY |

Sunday 30th June. Played at Yokohama (See Page 194)

Teams:

_____ | _____
_____ | _____
_____ | _____
_____ | _____
_____ | _____
_____ | _____
_____ | _____
_____ | _____
_____ | _____
_____ | _____
_____ | _____

Substitutes:

_____ | _____
_____ | _____

Goal Scorers:

_____ | _____
_____ | _____
_____ | _____
_____ | _____

Winners: | **Runners Up:**

FANFARE
2002 WORLD CUP
GUIDE

Notes